Life in FIELD

Hermut Geipel

Translated from the German by
Andrea Dutton-Kölbl

Nature notes by Lydia West

*This book will help you to
recognize some of the animals and
plants to be found in our fields.*

Young Library

First published as Lebendiges Feld
© Copyright 1988 Franz Schneider
Verlag, Munich

Published in England in 1989 by
Young Library Ltd
The Old Brushworks
56 Pickwick Road
Corsham, Wiltshire SN13 9BX

© Copyright 1989 Young Library Ltd
All rights reserved
ISBN 0 946003 15 7
Printed and bound in Hong Kong

A field is an enclosed piece of land where crops are cultivated. Sometimes the 'crop' is simply grass on which cows and sheep graze. Other animal fodder, such as hay, clover, and mangel wurzels, are cultivated in fields.

Most fields are used to grow food for our own consumption, such as grain and vegetables.

Fields also attract wild animals. They too find food there, and shelter among the tall crops. When the crops are harvested there is grain to be eaten, and millions of insects exposed to the eager eyes of birds. At the edges of fields dozens of wild flowers flourish, and bees and other insects flock to them. It is delightful to walk and picnic at the edges of fields.

Twenty or thirty years ago a farm might have had twelve fields with a different crop in each. But more and more food needs to be grown, and larger tractors and harvesters are used. These machines can be used properly only on very large fields. So those twelve fields are combined into only two or three, with a single crop.

Chemical weedkillers destroy wild flowers, and fertilizers can pollute nearby ponds and streams.

People are becoming more aware of these problems and how to deal with them. The area of field in our fold-out picture shows how wild and cultivated plants flourish together with animals in a modern field.

Here is a plant which has attracted twelve different creatures to it. How many of them can you recognize?

Bees, bumble bees, butterflies, moths, and other insects feed on nectar from the flowers.

Rabbits, caterpillars, and greenflies come to the plant to feed on the leaves.

Birds, mice, beetles, and ants eat the plants' seeds.

Plants also provide some insects with a place for breeding and rearing their young, as well as for preying on other insects.

There is more life below the ground than there is above it. Every tree and plant you see has roots in the earth. Millions of animals like earthworms, woodlice, centipedes, spiders, insect larvae, beetles, and bacteria make their homes in the soil.

You could find all the creatures below in a single square metre of fertile soil. They are listed on the right.

1 A grasshopper laying eggs
2 Slug
3 Earthworm
4 Churchyard beetle
5 Insect larva
6 Woodlouse
7 Centipede
8 Springtail

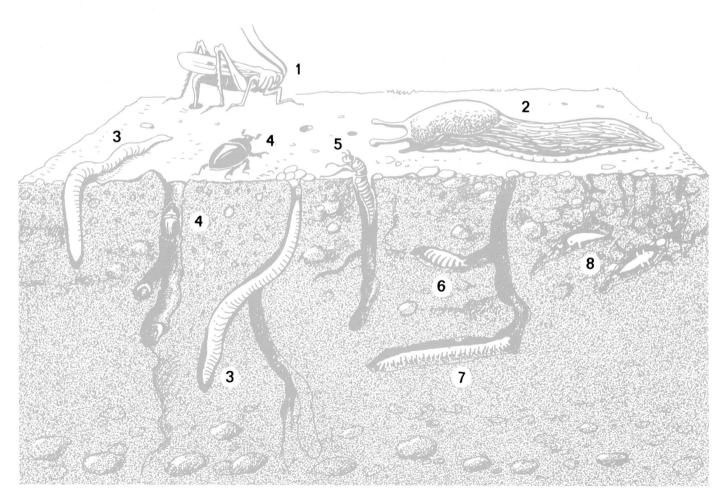

Nature Notes

The notes on the species are in the order of their names on the fold-out – from left to right of fold A, then B, and so on. The meaning of difficult words will be found in the Glossary on page 8.

Greater Plantain This plant grows up to 30cm, with broad leaves and dense spikes of tiny flowers. It flowers from April to August.

Goldfinch This 12cm bird perches on plants to pick out their seeds. It roosts in trees in flocks at night. In a nest lined with thistledown and often string which it unties from fruit bushes, it lays 5–6 bluish-white eggs with red spots 2–3 times a year.

Pill millipede This nocturnal invertebrate lives in soil or damp crevices feeding on decaying plants and root crops. Despite having dozens of pairs of legs it cannot run fast. When threatened it curls up into a tight ball.

Field pennycress This 15–60cm plant has round flat fruits, like pennies, and contains mustard oil. It flowers between May and July.

Mangel wurzel The big, swollen, fleshy roots of this crop are used as fodder for cattle and pigs. As the farmer wants only the roots, they are pulled up before the stems and flowers would appear in the second year.

Cabbage white and caterpillar This butterfly, 6cm across wings, often lays its bottle-shaped eggs on the underside of cabbage leaves. When the caterpillar hatches it feeds on the leaves. It then metamorphosizes into a butterfly which lives about four weeks.

Buzzard This 55cm bird of prey, with a 1m wingspan, is dark brown with paler underparts. It soars high in the air or sits on a high perch watching for rabbits and small animals. It nests on ledges or in trees and usually lays two eggs.

Black slug This 3–15cm mollusc is seen only at night or in the wet. It breathes through a hole in its back and smells through tentacles. It eats plants and small dead creatures. It lays 5mm amber eggs. It is covered in a slime which stops it drying out. You can tell where a slug has been by the slime-trails it leaves behind.

Common fumitory When pulled up, the roots of this plant smell smoky. Its small round fruits contain one seed each. It flowers from May to September, with 20–30 flowers on a stem. It grows up to 50cm.

Chickweed This plant is a favourite food of chickens and other poultry. It grows up to 36cm and can flower in mid-winter.

Horsefly This 11mm fly pierces the skin of horses and cattle to suck their blood. It also bites humans. The larvae live in damp soil and mud, and eat plant waste.

Brimstone When this hibernating insect with a 57mm wingspan folds its wings it looks like a pale leaf. The female is paler than the male. It feeds on the buckthorn where it lays its eggs and the caterpillars live until metamorphosis.

Whinchat This 13cm bird can be seen from April to September when it breeds in Britain. Its nest is hidden in thick ground cover. It can be seen on a perch, flicking its tail up and down, looking for flies or insects on the ground. It lays 5–7 greenish-blue eggs with brown speckles.

Tree sparrow This common 14cm bird eats mainly seeds, and can be a pest to farmers. In holes in trees, it makes a nest of grass or straw lined with feathers. It lays about four whitish brown-speckled eggs 2–3 times a year.

Maize Corn-on-the-cob, sweetcorn and popcorn come from the large yellow seed cobs of this sturdy 5m plant. Its most important uses are for breakfast cereals like cornflakes.

Fire bug Although rare in Britain, this hibernating 11mm insect can be seen in swarms on the ground in spring. It sucks seeds and feeds off dead animals.

Red clover The leaves are made

up of three leaflets; it is rare (and traditionally lucky!) to find a 4-leaved red clover. Growing up to 60cm it provides fodder for cattle, and is a favourite food of bees. It flowers from May to September.

Sexton beetle The 25mm 'Grave-digger' beetle can smell a dead creature up to two miles away. It buries it in a pit beneath the carcase, then returns to feed. The female lays eggs close by and the larvae feed off the same animal and its maggots. They are very important because they get rid of dead animals.

Bumble bee The 2cm queen builds an underground nest, usually from grass and moss. Worker bees collect pollen and nectar to feed the larvae and queen. Special males and females are hatched in late summer which mate; the females become queens. All the other bees die in autumn, while the new queens hibernate.

Brown hare By day the hare mainly lies in grass, feeding on cereals and grass in the evening and early morning. It has very good eyesight and hearing. Its long hind legs enable it to run at 35mph and to stand much higher than its 60cm length to peer about. It has litters of 2–4 young. Unlike rabbits hares don't live in burrows.

Colorado beetle and grub This 11mm beetle is rare in Britain and must be reported to the Police if seen because it is a serious potato pest. It hibernates in the ground, emerging to lay its yellow eggs on the potato plant. The larvae feed on the leaves for three weeks, then pupate in the ground.

Potato The underground stems of this plant have swellings called tubers, which are potatoes. Above ground the large, hairy leaves and stems grow 30–80cm. White or pale violet flowers appear between June and August.

Partridge You can recognise this 30cm bird by the horseshoe shape on its chest. Families live grouped together, eating seeds, berries, roots and sometimes ants. It nests under bushes or amongst tall plants and lays 8–23 brown pear-shaped eggs.

Common shrew This 12cm mammal spends three-quarters of its life underground and smells its way to the worms and insects which it must eat every three hours or else it will starve. It has two litters of about seven young, and lives about a year.

Skylark This 18cm migratory bird hovers very high, singing loudly. In its nest in the grass it lays 3–4 greenish-white speckled eggs. Its food is seeds, chickweed and small insects.

Potato (see entry on Fold C)
Colorado beetle (see entry on Fold C)
Shepherd's purse The heart-shaped fruit of this 8–45cm plant looks a bit like the purses shepherds used to carry. The seeds tumble out of the purse when ripe. This plant flowers all year round.

Goosegrass (cleavers) This plant (a favourite food of geese) grows to 130cm with whitish flowers from June to August. Its prickly leaves and fruit stick to animal hair and clothes.

Rape This member of the mustard family is cultivated for its seeds which give oil for cooking. The long narrow seed pods grow along the stem. It flowers from May to August and reaches over 1m. The bright yellow fields you see in the country are fields of rape.

Wild pansy Also known as Heartsease, this flower grows up to 30cm, blooming from April to September.

Barley This cereal plant, 130cm high, used mainly to feed cattle, is also used in making beer and whisky. The grains grow tightly together in spikes and it has a bearded appearance.

Charlock Also known as Field Mustard, charlock contains mustard oil in its seeds. The seed pods can lie dormant for many years, until the soil is broken up by ploughing. It flowers from May to July and grows up to 50cm.

Common hamster The burrows of this nocturnal hibernating rodent (about 13cm) are divided into separate nest and larder compartments. It collects cereals, roots etc in cheek pouches. It has

INTRODUCTION

- We have used colour sparingly in this guide and never purely for the sake of it.
  The text remains largely in black and white so that pages are spacious and uncluttered.
  All the summary questions are in black and white.

- Combining Higher and Foundation tiers allows the flexibility to reassess pupils at any time and therefore avoids categorising them too early in the course.

HIGHER TIER

- All Higher material is enclosed in a red box with the words 'HIGHER TIER' in the top right and bottom left hand corners. The Higher Tier material comprises about one third of the book and the great majority of this is confined to exclusively 'Higher' pages.

HIGHER TIER

- It's also important to realise that while the book is now 64 pages, the amount of material required to be revised remains the same as in our earlier editions. The same care has been taken to ensure that these notes are distilled to the essentials.

- As the originators of syllabus specific guides, we have remained true to our original principles ...

- The guide is written specifically for your syllabus and contains all of the information you do need to know ...
  ... and just as importantly, none of the information that you don't need to know!

- It still has an informal, user friendly style, and the content is divided into easy to learn sections.

- Key features are ...
  ... highlighted by boxes ...
  ... written in CAPITALS ...
  ... or emphasised by • bullet points.

  At the end of each page there is a short section containing revision exercises ...
  ... and at the end of each section there is a summary test in which the Higher Tier questions appear in red.

SOME IMPORTANT FACTS ABOUT YOUR EXAMINATION

- You will have THREE PAPERS, lasting 1 HOUR 30 MINUTES EACH.

- All papers will consist of COMPULSORY STRUCTURED QUESTIONS of different lengths, providing opportunity for extended prose writing and incorporating calculations and data response.

PAPER 1	LIFE AND LIVING PROCESSES.
PAPER 2	MATERIALS AND THEIR PROPERTIES.
PAPER 3	PHYSICAL PROCESSES.

CONTENTS

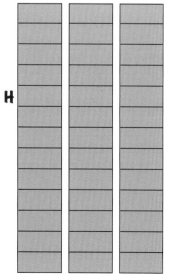

Covered in Class | Revised | Revised | Page No.

Classifying Materials

5   States of Matter I - Kinetic Theory. (6.1)
6   States of Matter II - Change of State. (6.1)
7   States of Matter III - Diffusion and Dissolving. (6.1)
8   Atomic Structure I - The Atom. (6.2)
9   Atomic Structure II - Electron Configuration. (6.2)
10 Bonding I - The Covalent Bond. (6.3)
11 Bonding II - Examples of Covalent Compounds. (6.3) **H**
12 Bonding III - The Ionic Bond. (6.3) *****
13 Bonding IV - Giant Structures. (6.3) **H**
14 Summary Questions.

Changing Materials

15 Useful Products from Oil I - Crude Oil. (7.1)
16 Useful Products from Oil II - Fractional Distillation, Cracking and Alkanes. (7.1) *****
17 Useful Products from Oil III - Alkenes and Polymers. (7.1) **H**
18 Useful Products from Metal Ores I - Iron (7.2)
19 Useful Products from Metal Ores II - Aluminium and Copper. (7.2) *****
20 Useful Products from Air I - Manufacture of Ammonia. (7.4)
21 Useful Products from Air II - Economics of the Haber Process. (8.7) **H**
22 Useful Products from Rocks (7.3)
23 Summary Questions.

Patterns of Behaviour

24 The Periodic Table I - Classification of Elements. (8.1)
25 The Periodic Table II - The Elements of Group I. (8.1)
26 The Periodic Table III - The Elements of Group 7. (8.1)
27 The Periodic Table IV - The Elements of Group 0 and the Transition Metals. (8.1)
28 The Periodic Table V - Trends in Reactivity. (8.1) **H**
29 Metals and Non-Metals I - Characteristics and Uses. (8.3)
30 Metals and Non-Metals II - The Reactivity Series. (8.3)
31 Metals and Non-Metals III - Displacement Reactions. (8.3)
32 Compounds of Alkali Metals and Halogens. (8.4)
33 Acids and Alkalis I - Indicators, pH Scale and Neutralisation. (8.2)
34 Acids and Alkalis II. (8.2)
35 Summary Questions.
36 Summary Questions.

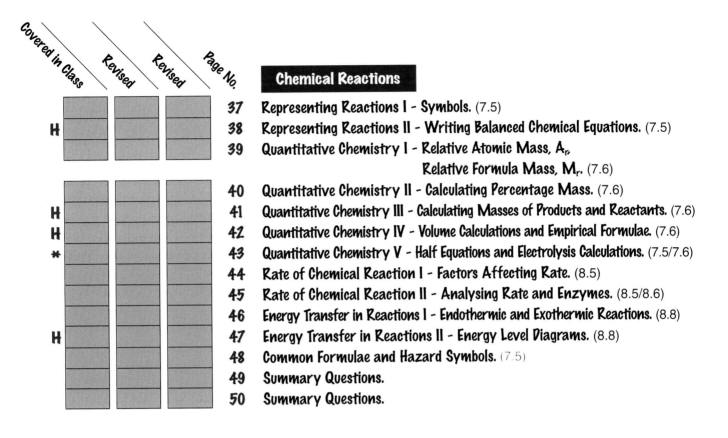

Covered in Class	Revised	Revised	Page No.	

Chemical Reactions

H

37 Representing Reactions I - Symbols. (7.5)
38 Representing Reactions II - Writing Balanced Chemical Equations. (7.5)
39 Quantitative Chemistry I - Relative Atomic Mass, A_r,
    Relative Formula Mass, M_r. (7.6)
40 Quantitative Chemistry II - Calculating Percentage Mass. (7.6)
H 41 Quantitative Chemistry III - Calculating Masses of Products and Reactants. (7.6)
H 42 Quantitative Chemistry IV - Volume Calculations and Empirical Formulae. (7.6)
✱ 43 Quantitative Chemistry V - Half Equations and Electrolysis Calculations. (7.5/7.6)
44 Rate of Chemical Reaction I - Factors Affecting Rate. (8.5)
45 Rate of Chemical Reaction II - Analysing Rate and Enzymes. (8.5/8.6)
46 Energy Transfer in Reactions I - Endothermic and Exothermic Reactions. (8.8)
H 47 Energy Transfer in Reactions II - Energy Level Diagrams. (8.8)
48 Common Formulae and Hazard Symbols. (7.5)
49 Summary Questions.
50 Summary Questions.

Earth Science

H

51 Changes to the Atmosphere I. (7.7)
52 Changes to the Atmosphere II. (7.7)
H 53 Changes to the Atmosphere III - Evolution of Atmosphere. (7.7)
54 Rock Types I - Formation, Characteristics and Specific Features. (7.8)
55 Rock Types II - The Rock Cycle. (7.8)
56 Tectonics I - The Earth. (7.9)
57 Tectonics II - Tectonic Plates. (7.9)
H 58 Tectonics III - Moving Plates. (7.9)
59 Summary Questions.

62 Index.
63 Index.

64 Periodic Table.

H - indicates HIGHER TIER material only.

✱ - indicates some HIGHER TIER material.

HOW TO USE THIS REVISION GUIDE

- Don't just read! LEARN ACTIVELY!

- Constantly test yourself ... WITHOUT LOOKING AT THE BOOK.

- When you have revised a small sub-section or a diagram, PLACE A BOLD TICK AGAINST IT. Similarly, tick the "progress and revision" section of the contents when you have done a page. This is great for your self confidence.

- Jot down anything which will help YOU to remember - no matter how trivial it may seem.

- DON'T BE TEMPTED TO HIGHLIGHT SECTIONS WITH DIFFERENT COLOURS. TOO MUCH COLOUR REDUCES CLARITY AND CAUSES CONFUSION. YOUR EXAM WILL BE IN BLACK AND WHITE!

- These notes are highly refined. Everything you need is here, in a highly organised but user friendly format. Many questions depend only on STRAIGHTFORWARD RECALL OF FACTS, so make sure you LEARN THEM.

HIGHER TIER

- Only those pupils doing HIGHER TIER should revise the material in the red boxes.

- THIS IS YOUR BOOK! Use it throughout your course in the ways suggested and your revision will be both organised and successful.

A WORD ABOUT THE LAYOUT OF THE CHEMISTRY GUIDE

Although the contents page links each page to its syllabus reference number, we have changed the layout to a more friendly form. The syllabus places everything in just 3 sections meaning that for instance 'Quantitative Chemistry' was lumped in with 'Rock Types', while 'Rates of Reaction' was in the same section as 'The Periodic Table'. By expanding the number of sections to 5 we have been able to put 'Quantitative Chemistry' and 'Rates of Reaction' in a separate group together with other similar themes. Also we have included the 'Earth Science' topics together. The page titles can be readily found in the syllabus and as stated above are cross-referenced to the syllabus reference number.

Classifying Materials

The KINETIC THEORY OF MATTER states that ...

- ... matter is made up of VERY SMALL PARTICLES (atoms, molecules, ions) ...
- ... which are CONTINUALLY MOVING.
- The extent of this movement depends on their STATE. ...
- ... and the TEMPERATURE they are at.

Let's look at the THREE STATES OF MATTER using Kinetic theory:

SOLIDS

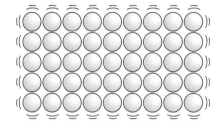

Particles are ...
- VERY CLOSE TOGETHER and ...
- ... EACH PARTICLE exerts a STRONG FORCE OF ATTRACTION ...
- ... on every OTHER PARTICLE.

Particles can ...
- ONLY VIBRATE (move to and fro) ...
- ... about a FIXED POSITION.

Solids have ...
- A DEFINITE VOLUME. (Take up a fixed amount of space)
- A DEFINITE SHAPE.

LIQUIDS

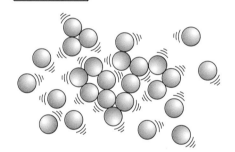

Particles are ...
- CLOSE TOGETHER and ...
- ... EACH PARTICLE exerts a SMALLER FORCE OF ATTRACTION ...
- ... on every OTHER PARTICLE.

Particles can ...
- MOVE AROUND ...
- ... in ANY DIRECTION within the liquid.

Liquids have ...
- A DEFINITE VOLUME.
- NO DEFINITE SHAPE. (They take up the shape of their container)

Liquids can ...
- BE POURED. (They flow)

GASES

Particles are ...
- VERY FAR APART and ...
- ... there is NO FORCE OF ATTRACTION ...
- ... between the PARTICLES.

Particles can ...
- MOVE AROUND QUICKLY ...
- ... in ANY DIRECTION ...
- ... within their container.

Gases have ...
- NO DEFINITE VOLUME.
- NO DEFINITE SHAPE.

Gases can ...
- BE COMPRESSED. (Squashed)
- FLOW.

- The Kinetic theory of matter states that matter is made up of very small particles which are continually moving.
- Solids have a definite volume and shape. • Liquids have a definite volume but not shape. They can be poured.
- Gases have no definite volume or shape. They can be compressed and they can flow.

- When the PARTICLES of a SUBSTANCE ...
    - ... GAIN or LOSE ENERGY ...
        - ... the substance MAY CHANGE ITS STATE.

Below is a graph of TEMPERATURE against TIME for a substance, initially in its SOLID STATE, which was SUPPLIED with HEAT ENERGY.

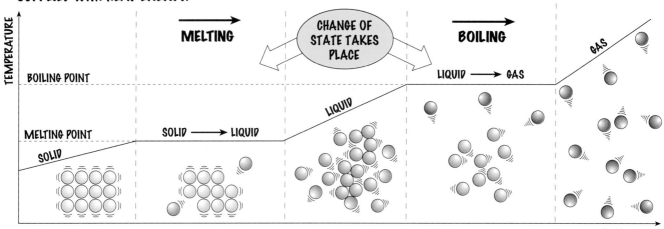

CHANGE OF STATE - The Kinetic Theory Explanation

1. SOLID TO LIQUID

When a SOLID ...
- ... is SUPPLIED with HEAT ENERGY ...
- ... its PARTICLES VIBRATE MORE AND MORE VIOLENTLY.
- If they have ENOUGH ENERGY ...
- ... they can OVERCOME the STRONG FORCES OF ATTRACTION, ...
- ... and break free from EACH OTHER ...
- They are now FREE TO MOVE AROUND.

When this happens ...
- ... the SOLID has become a LIQUID.
- This is MELTING and ...
- ... occurs at a TEMPERATURE called the MELTING POINT.

2. LIQUID TO GAS

When a LIQUID ...
- ... is SUPPLIED with HEAT ENERGY ...
- ... its PARTICLES MOVE AROUND MORE QUICKLY.
- If they have ENOUGH ENERGY ...
- ... they can OVERCOME the FORCES OF ATTRACTION, ...
- ... and escape from the liquid to become a GAS.
- This is EVAPORATION.

Evaporation is faster ...
- ... when the TEMPERATURE of the liquid is HIGHER.
- If the temperature is HIGH ENOUGH ...
- ... the liquid will BOIL.
- This occurs at a temperature called the BOILING POINT.

If the CHANGE OF STATE is in the OTHER DIRECTION ...
... i.e. GAS to LIQUID to SOLID ...
... the process is OPPOSITE TO THAT ABOVE.
Also ...
... if a GAS was being COOLED DOWN ...
... a graph of TEMP. against TIME would look like ...

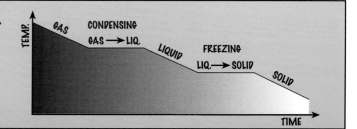

- The two possible changes of state are, melting and boiling for a substance which gains energy, and condensing and freezing for a substance which loses energy.

DIFFUSION

If you pass a fish and chip shop when it's nearly lunch time you can't fail to smell the delicious aroma of the food being prepared. The reason this happens is that PARTICLES of GAS given off by the food SPREAD OUT through the AIR. This is DIFFUSION.

Diffusion occurs when ...

- TWO DIFFERENT GASES (or LIQUIDS), MIX TOGETHER so that the CONCENTRATION OF THE TWO GASES (or LIQUIDS) ...
- ... eventually becomes the SAME EVERYWHERE, because the PARTICLES are CONSTANTLY MOVING.

Here are TWO JARS of GAS, ONE containing OXYGEN and the OTHER BROMINE (a brownish gas) ...

OXYGEN GAS (high concentration)

GAS JAR LIDS ARE REMOVED

BROMINE GAS (high concentration)

LATER

LATER

The concentration of both BROMINE and OXYGEN are now the same throughout the mixture.

... and the KINETIC THEORY EXPLANATION of how this happens ...

OXYGEN PARTICLES

BROMINE PARTICLES

SOME MIXING HAS TAKEN PLACE

PARTICLES COMPLETELY MIXED TOGETHER

- ALL GAS PARTICLES move around VERY QUICKLY in ALL DIRECTIONS.
- There is plenty of SPACE between the particles and so ...
- ... the GASES easily MIX INTO EACH OTHER, until they are evenly spread.
- The same effect can be seen using LIQUIDS but ...
- ... it happens more slowly.

DISSOLVING

A SUGAR LUMP has just been ADDED to a BEAKER OF WATER ...

LATER

LATER

... and the KINETIC THEORY EXPLANATION of how this happens ...

LIQUID PARTICLES (water molecules)

SOLID (sugar lump) CONSISTING OF PARTICLES

SOME DISSOLVING AND MIXING HAS TAKEN PLACE

SOLID COMPLETELY DISSOLVED AND PARTICLES COMPLETELY MIXED TOGETHER

- The LIQUID PARTICLES (in our example they are water molecules) are FREE TO MOVE AROUND.
- They COLLIDE with the SOLID or SOLUTE (the sugar lump) BREAKING OFF PARTICLES.
- The solid particles SPREAD OUT INTO THE LIQUID.
- This is DISSOLVING.

- Diffusion occurs when two different gases or liquids mix together so that the conc^n of the two gases or liquids becomes the same everywhere. • Dissolving occurs when liquid particles collide with a solid breaking off particles which then spread out.

All substances are made of atoms. A substance which contains only one sort of atom is called an ELEMENT. The atom is the basic building block of matter and consists of ...
- ... a small CENTRAL NUCLEUS ...
- ... made up of PROTONS and NEUTRONS (one exception!!) ...
- ... surrounded by ELECTRONS arranged in SHELLS. (ENERGY LEVELS)

A SIMPLE EXAMPLE – HELIUM

PROTON
- Positively charged.
- An atom has the same number of protons as electrons ...
... so the atom as a whole has no electrical charge.
- Same mass as a neutron.

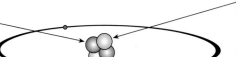

NEUTRON
- Neutral - no charge.
- Same mass as a proton.

ELECTRON
- Negatively charged.
- Same number of electrons as protons.
- Mass negligible i.e. nearly nothing!

ATOMIC PARTICLE	RELATIVE MASS	RELATIVE CHARGE
PROTON	1	+1
NEUTRON	1	0
ELECTRON	0 (nearly!)	-1

MASS NUMBER AND PROTON NUMBER

Atoms of an element can be described very conveniently; take the Helium atom above ...

MASS NUMBER

NUMBER OF PROTONS AND NEUTRONS

(everything that's in the nucleus!)

$$_2^4 \text{He}$$

ELEMENT SYMBOL

IN THIS CASE, THE ELEMENT HELIUM

PROTON NUMBER

NUMBER OF PROTONS ONLY

Here are some more elements in the periodic table.

ELEMENT	HYDROGEN	BORON	OXYGEN	ZINC	GOLD
SYMBOL	$_1^1 \text{H}$	$_5^{11} \text{B}$	$_8^{16} \text{O}$	$_{30}^{64} \text{Zn}$	$_{79}^{197} \text{Au}$
No. of PROTONS	1	5	8	30	79
No. of NEUTRONS	0 (the exception)	6	8	34	118
No. of ELECTRONS	1	5	8	30	79

ALWAYS THE SAME!

ISOTOPES

- ALL ATOMS of a particular ELEMENT have the SAME NUMBER OF PROTONS.
- Atoms of different elements have different numbers of protons.
- <u>The NUMBER of PROTONS, DEFINES THE ELEMENT.</u>
  - <u>HOWEVER</u>, some atoms of the SAME ELEMENT can have DIFFERENT NUMBERS OF NEUTRONS ...
    - ... these are called ISOTOPES.

EXAMPLE

Oxygen has 3 isotopes ...

$_8^{16}\text{O}$ ... has 8 neutrons ...

$_8^{17}\text{O}$ ... has 9 neutrons ...

$_8^{18}\text{O}$ ... has 10 neutrons ...

ALL ISOTOPES OF THE SAME ELEMENT HAVE THE SAME CHEMICAL PROPERTIES

- The atom is made up of a small central nucleus which contains protons and neutrons surrounded by electrons arranged in shells. • Isotopes are atoms of an element that have the same number of protons but a different number of neutrons.

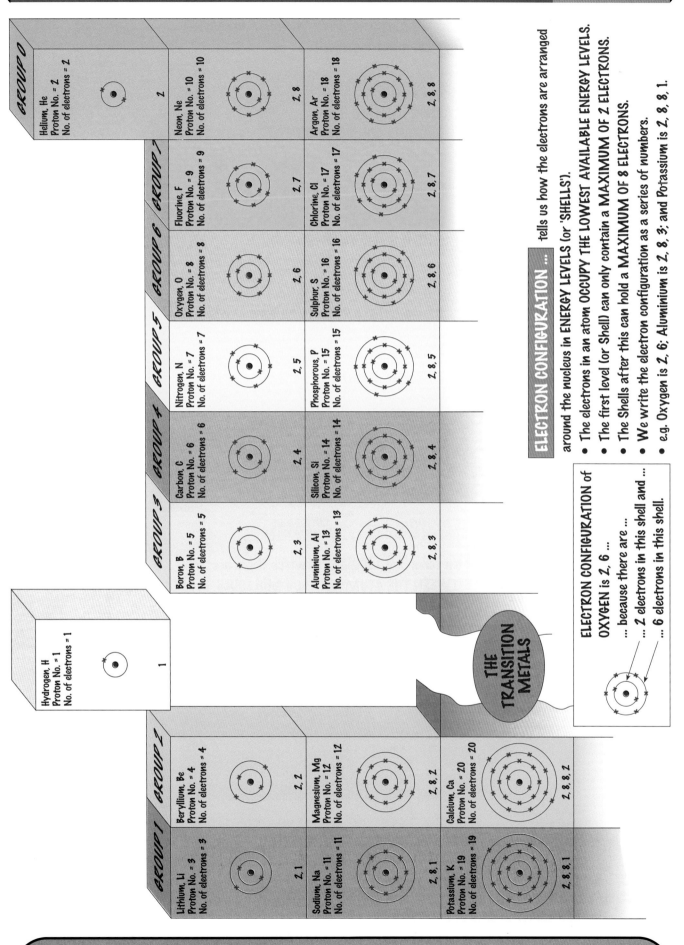

ELECTRON CONFIGURATION ... tells us how the electrons are arranged around the nucleus in ENERGY LEVELS (or 'SHELLS').

• The electrons in an atom OCCUPY THE LOWEST AVAILABLE ENERGY LEVELS.
• The first level (or Shell) can only contain a MAXIMUM OF 2 ELECTRONS.
• The Shells after this can hold a MAXIMUM OF 8 ELECTRONS.
• We write the electron configuration as a series of numbers.
• e.g. Oxygen is 2, 6; Aluminium is 2, 8, 3; and Potassium is 2, 8, 8, 1.

ELECTRON CONFIGURATION of OXYGEN is 2, 6 ...
... because there are ...
... 2 electrons in this shell and ...
... 6 electrons in this shell.

THE TRANSITION METALS

• Electrons are arranged in energy levels or shells.
• The first shell can contain a maximum of 2 electrons only.
• After this all other shells can contain a maximum of 8 electrons only.

- COMPOUNDS are substances in which the atoms of TWO OR MORE ELEMENTS ...
- ... are CHEMICALLY COMBINED (<u>not</u> just <u>mixed</u> together!).

ATOMS CAN FORM CHEMICAL BONDS BY EITHER ...
    ... (1) SHARING ELECTRONS (COVALENT BONDS), or ...
    ... (2) GAINING OR LOSING ELECTRONS (IONIC BONDS).

- Either way, when atoms form chemical bonds the arrangement of the <u>outermost</u> shell of electrons changes ...
- ... resulting in each atom getting a "<u>complete</u>" outer shell of electrons.
- For most atoms this is EIGHT ELECTRONS ...
- ... but for the FIVE LIGHTEST ELEMENTS it is only TWO! (See P.5).

1. THE COVALENT BOND

- Occurs between NON-METAL atoms and forms a very strong bond in which ELECTRONS ARE SHARED.

EXAMPLE

A CHLORINE MOLECULE (made of two chlorine atoms).

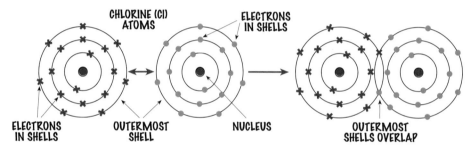

CHLORINE (Cl) ATOMS   ELECTRONS IN SHELLS

ELECTRONS IN SHELLS   OUTERMOST SHELL   NUCLEUS   OUTERMOST SHELLS OVERLAP

BOTH NOW HAVE 8 ELECTRONS IN OUTER SHELL. THEREFORE FULL SHELLS.

- Atoms which share electrons often form MOLECULES, in which there are ...
- ... STRONG CHEMICAL BONDS BETWEEN THE ATOMS IN EACH MOLECULE, but <u>NOT</u> between SEPARATE MOLECULES.

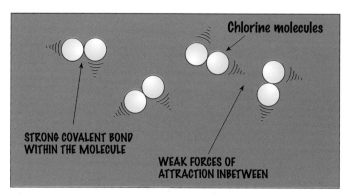

Chlorine molecules

STRONG COVALENT BOND WITHIN THE MOLECULE

WEAK FORCES OF ATTRACTION INBETWEEN

- This means they usually have LOW MELTING AND BOILING POINTS.

However ...
- ... atoms which share electrons can also form GIANT STRUCTURES e.g. DIAMOND (for diagram see P.13).
- They have HIGH MELTING AND BOILING POINTS.

> - A compound is a substance where the atoms of two or more elements have been chemically combined.
> - A covalent bond occurs between non-metal atoms where they share electrons and a very strong bond is formed.

OTHER EXAMPLES

The following examples are all stated on the syllabus. You need to know three different forms of representing the covalent bonds in each molecule. Two forms are given in the examples below.

1. WATER, H_2O
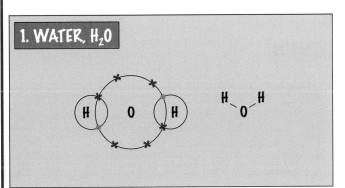

2. AMMONIA, NH_3
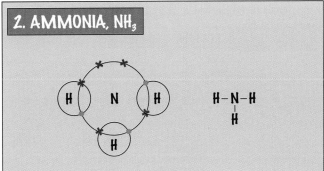

3. HYDROGEN, H_2
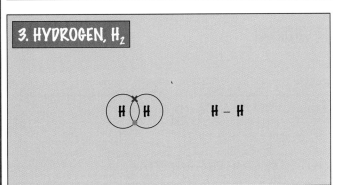

4. HYDROGEN CHLORIDE, HCl
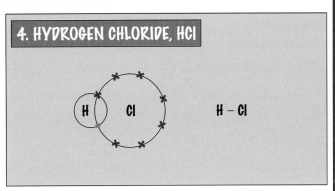

5. METHANE, CH_4
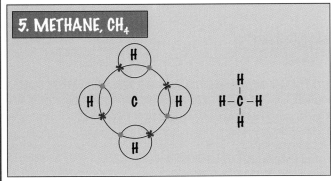

6. OXYGEN, O_2
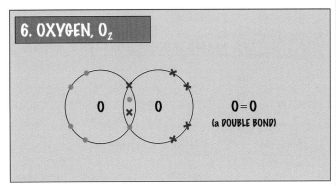

... the third form of representing covalent bonds is shown here for an Ammonia molecule.

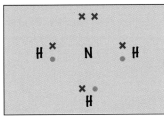

This is perhaps the most confusing method, and unless specifically asked for candidates should stick to the other two methods.

Simple covalent compounds ...

- ... have WEAK INTERMOLECULAR FORCES of ATTRACTION BETWEEN MOLECULES ...
- ... which results in them having LOW MELTING AND BOILING POINTS.
- They are NON-CONDUCTORS of ELECTRICITY as the molecules do not have an OVERALL ELECTRIC CHARGE.

HIGHER TIER

- Simple covalent compounds have weak intermolecular forces of attraction between molecules. This is why they have low melting and boiling points.
- They are also non-conductors of electricity since they have no overall electric charge.

2. THE IONIC BOND

- This occurs between a | METAL and a NON-METAL ATOM | ...
- ... and involves a | TRANSFER OF ELECTRONS | from one atom to the other ...
- ... to form electrically charged 'atoms' called | IONS | ...
- ... each of which has a "COMPLETE" OUTER ELECTRON SHELL.

EXAMPLE 1   SODIUM AND CHLORINE ... to form | SODIUM CHLORIDE. |

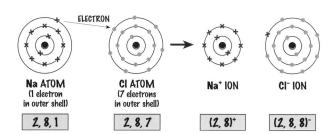

ELECTRON

Na ATOM
(1 electron
in outer shell)

2, 8, 1

Cl ATOM
(7 electrons
in outer shell)

2, 8, 7

Na⁺ ION

$(2, 8)^+$

Cl⁻ ION

$(2, 8, 8)^-$

- The SODIUM (Na) ATOM has 1 ELECTRON in its OUTER SHELL ...
- ... which is TRANSFERRED to the CHLORINE (Cl) ATOM.
- BOTH now have 8 ELECTRONS in their OUTER SHELL.
- The atoms are now | IONS | ...
- ... Na⁺ and Cl⁻ ...
- ... and the COMPOUND FORMED is ...
- ... SODIUM CHLORIDE, NaCl.

EXAMPLE 2   CALCIUM AND CHLORINE ... to form | CALCIUM CHLORIDE. |

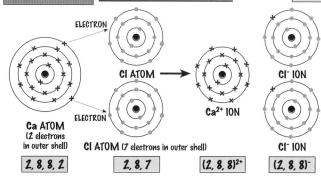

ELECTRON

Cl ATOM

Ca ATOM
(2 electrons
in outer shell)

2, 8, 8, 2

ELECTRON

Cl ATOM (7 electrons in outer shell)

2, 8, 7

Ca²⁺ ION

$(2, 8, 8)^{2+}$

Cl⁻ ION

Cl⁻ ION

$(2, 8, 8)^-$

- The CALCIUM (Ca) ATOM has 2 ELECTRONS in its OUTER SHELL.
- A CHLORINE (Cl) ATOM only 'WANTS' 1 ELECTRON ...
- ... therefore 2 Cl ATOMS ARE NEEDED.
- The atoms are now | IONS | ...
- ... Ca²⁺, Cl⁻ and Cl⁻ ...
- ... and the COMPOUND FORMED is ...
- ... CALCIUM CHLORIDE, CaCl₂.

EXAMPLE 3   MAGNESIUM AND OXYGEN ... to form | MAGNESIUM OXIDE. |

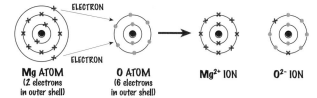

ELECTRON

Mg ATOM
(2 electrons
in outer shell)

2, 8, 2

ELECTRON

O ATOM
(6 electrons
in outer shell)

2, 6

Mg²⁺ ION

$(2, 8)^{2+}$

O²⁻ ION

$(2, 8)^{2-}$

- The MAGNESIUM (Mg) ATOM has 2 ELECTRONS in its OUTER SHELL ...
- ... which are TRANSFERRED to the OXYGEN (O) ATOM.
- BOTH now have 8 ELECTRONS in their OUTER SHELL.
- The atoms are now | IONS | ...
- ... Mg²⁺ and O²⁻ ...
- ... and the COMPOUND FORMED is ...
- ... MAGNESIUM OXIDE, Mg O.

N.B.   IONIC COMPOUNDS ARE GIANT STRUCTURES OF IONS ...
... WITH HIGH MELTING AND BOILING POINTS (for diagram see below).

HIGHER TIER

STRUCTURE OF IONIC COMPOUNDS

Ionic compounds form ...
- ... REGULAR STRUCTURES (GIANT IONIC LATTICES) ...
- ... with STRONG FORCES OF ATTRACTION ...
- ... BETWEEN ADJACENT IONS resulting in ...
- ... them having HIGH MELTING and BOILING POINTS.

Ionic compounds ...
- ... CONDUCT ELECTRICITY when they are ...
- ... MOLTEN or DISSOLVED IN WATER due to ...
- ... the IONS which are now FREE TO MOVE.

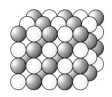

◐ POSITIVELY CHARGED IONS
(atoms which have lost electrons).

○ NEGATIVELY CHARGED IONS
(atoms which have gained electrons).

HIGHER TIER

- An ionic bond occurs between a metal and a non-metal atom where there is a transfer of electrons from one atom to the other. These electrically charged atoms are called ions.
- Ionic compounds are giant structures of ions with high melting and boiling points. They also conduct electricity.

DIAMOND (A FORM OF CARBON)

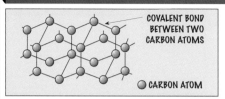

COVALENT BOND BETWEEN TWO CARBON ATOMS

CARBON ATOM

- A **GIANT, RIGID COVALENT STRUCTURE (LATTICE)** where EACH CARBON ATOM ...
- ... forms **FOUR** COVALENT BONDS with OTHER CARBON ATOMS.
- The LARGE NUMBER of COVALENT BONDS results in diamond having a VERY HIGH MELTING POINT.

GRAPHITE (A FORM OF CARBON)

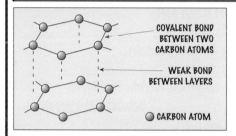

COVALENT BOND BETWEEN TWO CARBON ATOMS

WEAK BOND BETWEEN LAYERS

CARBON ATOM

- A **GIANT, COVALENT STRUCTURE (LATTICE)** in which EACH CARBON ATOM ...
- ... forms **THREE** COVALENT BONDS with OTHER CARBON ATOMS ...
- ... in a LAYERED STRUCTURE which can SLIDE PAST EACH OTHER.
- Between LAYERS there are WEAK FORCES of ATTRACTION ...
- ... resulting in FREE ELECTRONS and so graphite CONDUCTS ELECTRICITY.

SILICON DIOXIDE, SO$_2$ (SILICA)

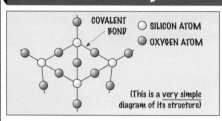

COVALENT BOND

SILICON ATOM
OXYGEN ATOM

(This is a very simple diagram of its structure)

- A **GIANT COVALENT STRUCTURE (LATTICE)** similar to diamond where EACH OXYGEN ATOM is JOINED ...
- ... to TWO SILICON ATOMS and each SILICON ATOM is JOINED to FOUR OXYGEN ATOMS.
- The LARGE NUMBER of COVALENT BONDS results in silicon dioxide having a VERY HIGH MELTING POINT.

METALS

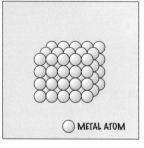

METAL ATOM

- Form **GIANT STRUCTURES** with ELECTRONS from the OUTERMOST ENERGY LEVELS FREE TO MOVE THROUGH the STRUCTURE.
- These electrons ...
- ... ATTRACT the POSITIVE METAL IONS, holding them together in a REGULAR STRUCTURE.
- ... ALLOW the ATOMS to SLIDE PAST EACH OTHER and so metals are MALLEABLE and DUCTILE.
- ... ALLOW CONDUCTION of HEAT and ELECTRICITY.

PLASTICS

- PLASTICS are a TANGLED MASS of VERY LONG MOLECULES ...
- ... in which the ATOMS are joined by STRONG COVALENT BONDS to form LONG CHAINS called POLYMERS.

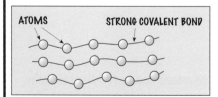

ATOMS   STRONG COVALENT BOND

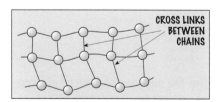

CROSS LINKS BETWEEN CHAINS

A **THERMOSOFTENING PLASTIC** will ...
- ... SOFTEN when HEATED and HARDEN when COOLED as the ...
- ... FORCES between CHAINS are WEAK.
- THESE PLASTICS CAN BE MOULDED.

A **THERMOSETTING PLASTIC** will ...
- ... WHEN HEATED form COVALENT BONDS between ADJACENT CHAINS ...
- ... causing STRONG CROSS LINKS which mean ...
- ... that the plastics will NOT SOFTEN when REHEATED.
- THESE PLASTICS CANNOT BE REMOULDED.

HIGHER TIER

- Diamond, graphite and silicon dioxide are all giant covalent structures.
- Metals also form giant structures.
- There are two types of plastic: thermosoftening and thermosetting

1. In the spaces below draw diagrams to show how the particles are arranged in a) a solid b) a liquid and c) a gas.

a)

b)

c)

2. Fill in the spaces below using the following words (use each one only <u>once</u>) MOVE AROUND, FAR APART, VERY CLOSE TOGETHER, VIBRATE, SMALLER FORCE OF ATTRACTION, MOVE AROUND QUICKLY, CLOSE TOGETHER, STRONG FORCE OF ATTRACTION, NO FORCE OF ATTRACTION.
   a) In a solid the particles are _____ and each particle exerts a _____ on every other particle. The particles can only_____ about a fixed position.
   b) In a liquid the particles are _____ and each particle exerts a _____ on every other particle. The particles can _____ in any direction within the liquid.
   c) In a gas the particles_____ and there is_____ between the particles. The particles can_____ in any direction within their container.

3. Explain using the Kinetic theory how a) a solid can change into a liquid and b) a liquid can change into a gas.

4. a) What is diffusion? Explain your answer by drawing diagrams showing two gas jars, one filled with bromine gas and the other with oxygen gas. b) Draw diagrams to help you explain the Kinetic theory explanation of what has happened in part a).

5. Fill in the spaces below using the following words: (use each one only once)
   ELECTRONS, CENTRAL NUCLEUS, ELEMENT, NEUTRONS, ATOM, PROTONS, SHELLS.
   All substances are made of atoms. A substance which contains only one sort of _____ is called an _____ . The atom consists of a small _____ made up of_____ and _____ surrounded by _____ arranged in _____ .

6. a) What are isotopes?
   b) Here are three isotopes for oxygen. $^{16}_{8}O$ $^{17}_{8}O$ $^{18}_{8}O$
   Which isotope (i) contains 9 neutrons? (ii) is the heaviest? (iii) contains 8 protons?

7. Draw diagrams to show the electron configurations for the following atoms a) Carbon b) Aluminium c) Chlorine and d) Potassium.

8. a) What is the difference between a covalent and an ionic bond?
   b) Draw diagrams to show how a chlorine molecule is made from two chlorine atoms.
   c) The diagram below shows an incomplete diagram of the ionic bond which occurs between a sodium atom and a chlorine atom. Copy and complete the diagram.

   Na ATOM
   2, 8, 1

   Cl ATOM
   2, 8, 7

9. Draw diagrams, showing the outermost shell of electrons only, to show the covalent bonds for the following compounds a) Water b) Methane and c) Oxygen.

10. Below is a simple diagram showing the structure of an ionic compound.
    Explain why ...

    ● POSITIVELY CHARGED IONS
    ○ NEGATIVELY CHARGED IONS

    a) Ionic compounds have high melting and boiling points b) Ionic compounds conduct electricity.

11. Explain why a) a diamond has a very high melting point b) graphite conducts electricity c) silicon dioxide has a very high melting point d) metals are conductors of electricity e) a thermosetting plastic cannot be remoulded.

Changing Materials

HOW CRUDE OIL IS FORMED

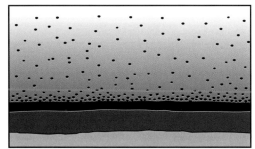

- Formed over millions of years from dead ORGANISMS ...
- ... mainly PLANKTON (tiny sea creatures) ...
- ... which fell to the ocean floor...
- ... and were covered by MUD SEDIMENTS.

- It is a FOSSIL FUEL.

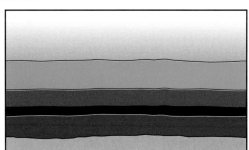

- Action of HEAT and PRESSURE ...
- ... in the ABSENCE OF OXYGEN ...
- ... caused the production of CRUDE OIL ...
- ... which becomes trapped between ...
- ... NON-POROUS layers of sediment.

- The oil remained underground (in most cases), ...
- ... TRAPPED in a LAYER OF POROUS ROCK ...
- ... sandwiched between TWO LAYERS OF NON-POROUS ROCK ...
- ... until oil exploration companies drilled down ...
- ... and 'released it'.
- The oil comes to the surface due to the pressure ...
- ... of the natural gas associated with it.

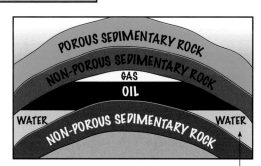

- COAL , another FOSSIL FUEL, is formed very similarly ...
- ... from the remains of dead PLANTS ...
- ... which were covered by MUD SEDIMENTS etc.

OIL AND GAS ARE LESS DENSE THAN WATER ... AND SO THEY RISE TO THE TOP OF THE POROUS ROCK LAYER

WHAT CRUDE OIL IS

- Crude oil is a mixture of compounds most of which ...
- ... are MOLECULES made up of CARBON and HYDROGEN atoms only, called HYDROCARBONS.

These hydrocarbon molecules vary in size. This affects their properties ...

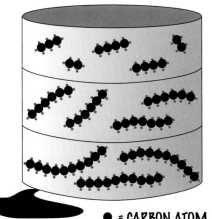

The LARGER the HYDROCARBON:
- the LESS EASILY it FLOWS ...
  ... i.e. the more viscous it is.
- the LESS EASILY it IGNITES ...
  ... i.e. the less flammable it is.
- the LESS VOLATILE it is ...
  ... i.e. it doesn't vaporise as easily.
- the HIGHER IT'S BOILING POINT.

● = CARBON ATOM   · = HYDROGEN ATOM

- Crude oil (a fossil fuel) is mainly made of molecules containing carbon and hydrogen atoms only called hydrocarbons.

FRACTIONAL DISTILLATION OF CRUDE OIL

Crude oil on it's own isn't a great deal of use. We need to separate it into it's different FRACTIONS all of which have their own PARTICULAR CHARACTERISTICS.

It is possible to separate crude oil into its FRACTIONS by ...
- ... EVAPORATING the oil by heating ...
- ... and then allowing it to CONDENSE ...
- ... at a RANGE of DIFFERENT TEMPERATURES ...
- ... when it will form FRACTIONS each of which ...
- ... will contain molecules ...
- ... with a SIMILAR NUMBER OF CARBON ATOMS.

- This is called FRACTIONAL DISTILLATION ...
- ... and is done in a FRACTIONATING COLUMN.

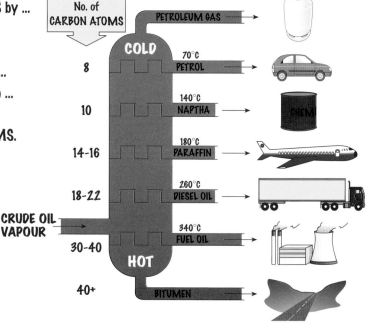

CRACKING

Because the SHORTER CHAIN HYDROCARBONS release energy more quickly by BURNING, there is a greater demand for them.
- Therefore LONGER CHAIN HYDROCARBONS are 'CRACKED' or broken down ...

- ... to produce SHORTER CHAIN HYDROCARBONS.
- Some of these are used as FUELS ...
- ... and some to make PLASTICS such as ...
- ... POLY(ETHENE) ...   ... and PVC.

Plastic Bowls   Plastic Bags   Wellington Boots   Electrical Insulation

HIGHER TIER

ALKANES - Saturated Hydrocarbons

- The 'SPINE' of a HYDROCARBON is made up of a chain of CARBON ATOMS.
- When EACH CARBON ATOM in the 'spine' forms FOUR SINGLE COVALENT BONDS ...
- ... we say the HYDROCARBON is SATURATED and it is known as an ALKANE.

Examples of Alkanes

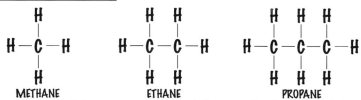

METHANE   ETHANE   PROPANE

- ALL THE CARBON ATOMS ARE LINKED TO 4 OTHER ATOMS.
- THEY ARE ALL 'FULLY OCCUPIED' OR SATURATED.
- ALL THE BONDS ARE SINGLE COVALENT BONDS.

Because all their bonds are 'occupied' they are fairly UNREACTIVE although they do burn well.

- Crude oil is separated into its fractions by fractional distillation and cracking is used to break down long chain hydrocarbons into short chain hydrocarbons. • Alkanes are saturated hydrocarbons.

ALKENES – Unsaturated Hydrocarbons

- Carbon atoms can also form DOUBLE COVALENT BONDS with other atoms.
- When the CARBON ATOMS in the 'spine' of a hydrocarbon have ...
- ... at least ONE DOUBLE COVALENT BOND, ...
- ... we say the HYDROCARBON is UNSATURATED and it is known as an ALKENE.

Examples of Alkenes

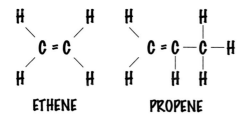

ETHENE   PROPENE

• NOT ALL THE CARBON ATOMS ARE LINKED TO 4 OTHER ATOMS.
• THEY ARE NOT ALL 'FULLY OCCUPIED' i.e. THEY ARE UNSATURATED.
• A DOUBLE BOND IS PRESENT.

Because of this DOUBLE BOND (=) the ALKENES have the potential to join with other atoms and so they are REACTIVE. This makes them useful for making other molecules, especially POLYMERS.

POLYMERS

- The small alkene molecules above can be described as MONOMERS
- When lots of MONOMERS join together they form a POLYMER.
- Because ALKENES are UNSATURATED, they are very good at joining together and ...
- ... when they do so <u>without producing another substance</u>, we call this ...
- ... ADDITION POLYMERISATION.

An example of Addition Polymerisation - Poly(ethene) (often called polythene)

$$H_2C=CH_2 + H_2C=CH_2 + H_2C=CH_2 + \text{thousands more} \longrightarrow$$

ethene monomers (unsaturated)   poly(ethene) polymer (saturated)

General formula for Addition Polymerisation

This can be applied to any ADDITION POLYMERISATION ...
... to represent the formation of a simple addition polymer.

$$n\left(\begin{array}{c} | \\ C = C \\ | \end{array}\right) \longrightarrow \left(\begin{array}{c} | \\ C - C \\ | \end{array}\right)_n$$

Where 'n' is a very large number.

- Alkenes are unsaturated hydrocarbons.
- Addition Polymerisation is the joining together of small alkene molecules without the production of another substance.

The Earth's crust contains many different METALS and METAL COMPOUNDS mixed in with other substances. A metal or metal compound found in enough concentration so that economically viable amounts of the metal can be extracted, is an ORE.

- Most ores are often the OXIDES of metals or substances that can easily be changed into a metal oxide.
- To extract the metal OXYGEN MUST BE REMOVED from the metal oxide.
- This is REDUCTION and the method of EXTRACTION ...
- ... depends on the <u>POSITION</u> of the metal in the REACTIVITY SERIES. (See P.30)

POSITION OF METAL	EXTRACTION PROCESS	EXAMPLES
Metals HIGH in the series (i.e. ABOVE CARBON) ...	... are extracted by ELECTROLYSIS.	ALUMINIUM, Magnesium, Sodium.
Metals in the MIDDLE of the series (i.e. BELOW CARBON) ...	... are extracted by HEATING WITH CARBON.	IRON, Lead, Copper.
Metals VERY LOW in the series ...	... are so UNREACTIVE they exist NATURALLY and NO EXTRACTION IS NEEDED.	GOLD, Platinum.

EXTRACTION OF IRON – The Blast Furnace

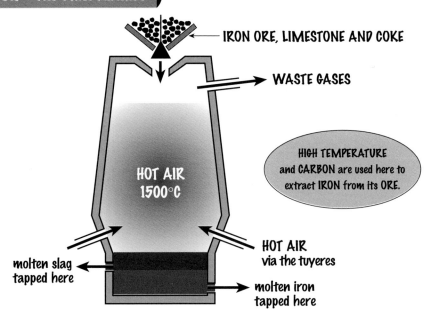

IRON ORE, LIMESTONE AND COKE

WASTE GASES

HIGH TEMPERATURE and CARBON are used here to extract IRON from its ORE.

HOT AIR 1500°C

HOT AIR via the tuyeres

molten slag tapped here

molten iron tapped here

- IRON ORE, LIMESTONE and COKE (CARBON) are fed into the top of the furnace.
- HOT AIR is BLASTED through the furnace via the TUYERES
- OXYGEN from this air reacts with the coke to form CARBON DIOXIDE
- CARBON DIOXIDE reacts with more coke to form CARBON MONOXIDE.

Now at these temperatures CARBON MONOXIDE will very quickly change to CARBON DIOXIDE by taking OXYGEN from the IRON OXIDE

IRON OXIDE + CARBON MONOXIDE ⟶ IRON + CARBON DIOXIDE

Carbon itself is often used to reduce oxides as it is quite high in the reactivity series. However, here it is CARBON MONOXIDE which acts as the REDUCING AGENT.

- The limestone ends up removing certain impurities (especially sand) by combining with it to form SLAG which is then run off.

- Metals above carbon in the reactivity series are extracted by electrolysis.
- Metals in the middle of the series are extracted by heating with carbon. • Metals very low in the series exist naturally.

Metals high in the REACTIVITY SERIES (i.e. <u>ABOVE CARBON</u>) are extracted by ELECTROLYSIS.
- ELECTROLYSIS is the breaking down of a compound ...
  - ... containing IONS ...
    - ... into its ELEMENTS ...
      - ... by using an ELECTRIC CURRENT.
- IONS are atoms or groups of atoms which have an ELECTRICAL CHARGE (+ or -)

EXTRACTION OF ALUMINIUM BY ELECTROLYSIS

- The RAW MATERIALS are ...
  ... PURIFIED ALUMINIUM OXIDE and CRYOLITE.
- The ALUMINIUM OXIDE is dissolved in <u>MOLTEN</u> CRYOLITE at about 850°C, ...
  ... the temperature would have to be much higher if we used just the oxide!
- The ELECTRODES are made of CARBON (graphite) which are used only to conduct the electricity, ...
  ... they don't take any part in the extraction.

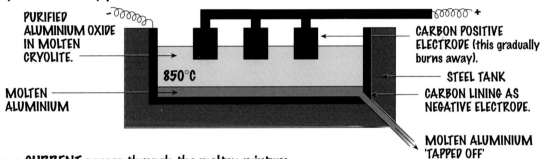

PURIFIED ALUMINIUM OXIDE IN MOLTEN CRYOLITE.

MOLTEN ALUMINIUM

850°C

CARBON POSITIVE ELECTRODE (this gradually burns away).

STEEL TANK

CARBON LINING AS NEGATIVE ELECTRODE.

MOLTEN ALUMINIUM 'TAPPED OFF'

- When a CURRENT passes through the molten mixture ...
- ... AT THE NEGATIVE ELECTRODE ...
- ... POSITIVELY CHARGED ALUMINIUM IONS MOVE TOWARDS IT and ALUMINIUM FORMS and ...
- ... AT THE POSITIVE ELECTRODES ...
- ... NEGATIVELY CHARGED OXYGEN IONS MOVE TOWARDS THEM and OXYGEN FORMS.
- This causes the positive electrodes to burn away quickly and they frequently have to be replaced.

PURIFICATION OF COPPER BY ELECTROLYSIS

Copper can easily be extracted by REDUCTION but when it is needed in a pure form it is purified by ELECTROLYSIS.

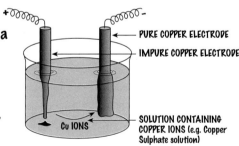

PURE COPPER ELECTRODE

IMPURE COPPER ELECTRODE

Cu IONS

SOLUTION CONTAINING COPPER IONS (e.g. Copper Sulphate solution)

- The POSITIVE ELECTRODE is made of IMPURE COPPER.
- AT THE POSITIVE ELECTRODE COPPER IONS pass into the solution.
- AT THE NEGATIVE ELECTRODE COPPER IONS MOVE TOWARDS IT ...
  ... TO FORM COPPER ATOMS ...
  ... which stick to the pure copper electrode.
- The impurities fall to the bottom as the IMPURE POSITIVE ELECTRODE GRADUALLY DISSOLVES.

HIGHER TIER

REDOX REACTIONS

During electrolysis ...
- ... at the NEGATIVE ELECTRODE POSITIVELY CHARGED IONS <u>GAIN</u> ELECTRONS.
- This gain of electrons is known as <u>REDUCTION</u>.
- At the POSITIVE ELECTRODE NEGATIVELY CHARGED IONS <u>LOSE</u> ELECTRONS.
- This loss of electrons is known as <u>OXIDATION</u>.
- A chemical reaction where <u>BOTH</u> REDUCTION and OXIDATION occurs is called a REDOX REACTION.

HIGHER TIER

- Electrolysis is the breaking down of a compound containing ions into its elements using an electric current.
- A chemical reaction where both reduction and oxidation occurs is called a Redox reaction.

The production of Ammonia and Nitric acid are intermediate steps in the production of Ammonium nitrate fertiliser. Until 1908 Nitrogen couldn't be turned into nitrates on a large scale, and the world was quickly running out of fertilisers! Even though air is almost 80% nitrogen!

STAGE 1: PRODUCTION OF AMMONIA - The Haber Process

The big breakthrough came in 1908 when Fritz Haber showed that Ammonia, a COLOURLESS, PUNGENT, ALKALINE GAS could be made on a large scale.

The Raw materials are:-
- NITROGEN - from the fractional distillation of liquid air.
- HYDROGEN - from Natural gas and steam.

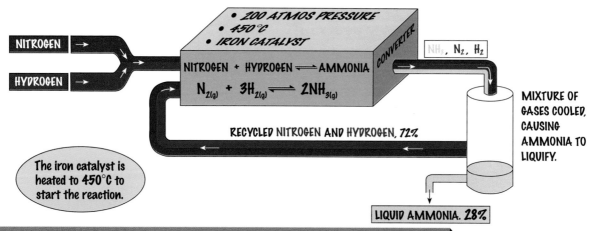

- 200 ATMOS PRESSURE
- 450°C
- IRON CATALYST

NITROGEN + HYDROGEN ⇌ AMMONIA
$$N_{2(g)} + 3H_{2(g)} \rightleftharpoons 2NH_{3(g)}$$

CONVERTER

NH_3, N_2, H_2

RECYCLED NITROGEN AND HYDROGEN, 72%

The iron catalyst is heated to 450°C to start the reaction.

MIXTURE OF GASES COOLED, CAUSING AMMONIA TO LIQUIFY.

LIQUID AMMONIA. 28%

STAGE 2: PRODUCTION OF NITRIC ACID - The Oxidation of Ammonia

The process involves two reactions, both of them involving OXYGEN.

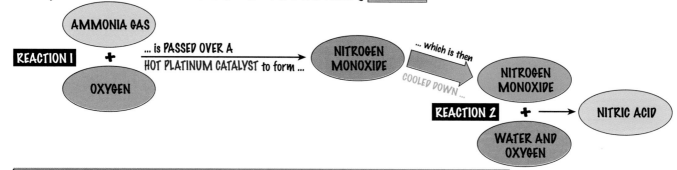

REACTION 1

AMMONIA GAS + OXYGEN

... is PASSED OVER A HOT PLATINUM CATALYST to form ...

NITROGEN MONOXIDE

... which is then COOLED DOWN ...

NITROGEN MONOXIDE

REACTION 2 + WATER AND OXYGEN → NITRIC ACID

STAGE 3: PRODUCTION OF AMMONIUM NITRATE - An important Fertiliser

- Although concentrated ammonia could be used as a fertiliser ...
- ... it is better to store SOLID FERTILISERS such as AMMONIUM NITRATE, NH_4NO_3.
- This as you can see is rich in NITROGEN ...
- ... and is sometimes known as 'NITRAM' (Nitrate of ammonia).

- Ammonium nitrate is made by reacting together ...
- ... AQUEOUS SOLUTIONS OF AMMONIA AND NITRIC ACID.
- This is an example of a <u>neutralisation reaction</u>.

'NITRAM' FERTILISER

| Ammonia | + | Nitric Acid | → | Ammonium Nitrate | This is then |
| $NH_{3(aq)}$ | + | $HNO_{3(aq)}$ | → | $NH_4NO_{3(aq)}$ | EVAPORATED TO DRYNESS |

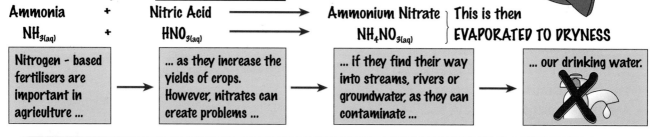

Nitrogen - based fertilisers are important in agriculture ... → ... as they increase the yields of crops. However, nitrates can create problems ... → ... if they find their way into streams, rivers or groundwater, as they can contaminate ... → ... our drinking water.

- The raw materials for the production of ammonia are nitrogen and hydrogen. • Nitrogen + Hydrogen ⇌ Ammonia.
- Ammonia reacts with oxygen first and then water and more oxygen to produce Nitric Acid.
- Aqueous solutions of Nitric Acid and Ammonia are then reacted together to produce Ammonium Nitrate.

There is great economic importance attached to getting the MAXIMUM AMOUNT of AMMONIA in the SHORTEST POSSIBLE TIME. This demands a degree of COMPROMISE.

EFFECT OF ENERGY TRANSFER, RATES OF REACTION AND EQUILIBRIUM CONDITIONS ON REVERSIBLE REACTIONS

The manufacture of AMMONIA is a **REVERSIBLE REACTION,** involving ...
- ENERGY TRANSFERS associated with the breaking and formation of chemical bonds.

ENDOTHERMIC ⟨ N_2 + $3H_2$ $\underset{\text{REVERSE}}{\overset{\text{FORWARD}}{\rightleftharpoons}}$ $2NH_3$ ⟩ EXOTHERMIC

In a CLOSED SYSTEM, AT EQUILIBRIUM, ...
- ... there is the SAME RATE OF REACTION IN EACH DIRECTION ...
- ... but, the RELATIVE AMOUNTS OF THE REACTANTS depend on ...
  ... the CONDITIONS OF THE REACTION.

Let's consider these three bullet points separately ...

1) ENERGY TRANSFERS DUE TO BREAKING AND FORMING OF CHEMICAL BONDS. (See P.46)
- Energy is needed in order to break the bonds in the Nitrogen and hydrogen molecules.
- Energy is given out in the formation of the bonds in the Ammonia molecule.
- In the FORWARD REACTION, more energy is released during BOND FORMATION, ...
- ... and so the reaction is EXOTHERMIC, and ENERGY IS TRANSFERRED TO THE SURROUNDINGS.

2) RATE OF REACTION. (See P.44/45)
- Increasing the temperature increases the RATE OF REACTION, EQUALLY for ..
- ... BOTH THE FORWARD and REVERSE REACTION.

3) EQUILIBRIUM CONDITIONS AND THEIR EFFECT ON YIELD.
TEMPERATURE has an important role to play, since this is an EXOTHERMIC reaction.
- In exothermic reactions, ... DECREASING THE TEMPERATURE ...
- ... MOVES THE EQUILIBRIUM to the RIGHT (in favour of the forward reaction) ...
- ... thereby INCREASING THE YIELD OF PRODUCTS (Ammonia in this case!)
- INCREASING THE TEMPERATURE would move the equilibrium to the left ...
- ... in favour of the ENDOTHERMIC REACTION. (i.e. production of N_2 + H_2)

A COMPROMISE SOLUTION

In reality, <u>A LOW TEMPERATURE INCREASES YIELD BUT THE REACTION IS TOO SLOW.</u>

So, a COMPROMISE is reached in the Haber process ...

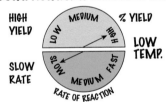

450°C is used as a COMPROMISE SOLUTION.

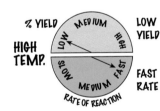

... while also ... CONCENTRATION or in this case PRESSURE also has an important role.
- INCREASING THE PRESSURE, favours the reaction which results in a reduction in volume ...
- ... and therefore MOVES THE EQUILIBRIUM to the RIGHT ... INCREASING THE YIELD ...
- ... as the VOLUME OF AMMONIA PRODUCED is LESS ...
- ... than the TOTAL VOLUME of NITROGEN and HYDROGEN which react to produce it.

In reality, <u>A HIGH PRESSURE INCREASES YIELD BUT THE REACTION IS TOO EXPENSIVE.</u>

So, yet again, a COMPROMISE is reached ...

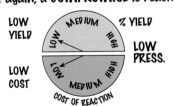

200 ATMOS.PRESS. is used as a COMPROMISE SOLUTION.

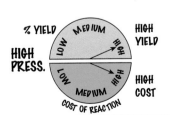

- The manufacture of ammonia is a reversible reaction. • N_2 + $3H_2$ $\rightleftharpoons$ $2NH_3$
- If the reaction is carried out at a low temperature, the yield is high but the reaction is too slow. A temperature of 450°C is used as a compromise. • Similarly high pressure gives a high yield but the reaction is too expensive. A pressure of 200 atmos. is used as a compromise.

HIGHER TIER

LIMESTONE

Limestone is a SEDIMENTARY ROCK consisting mainly of CALCIUM CARBONATE.
It is cheap, easy to obtain and has many uses:

1. NEUTRALISING AGENT

- Excess ACIDITY of soils can cause crop failure.
  - Alkalis can be 'washed out' by acid rain.
    - Powdered limestone can correct this ...
      - ... but it works quite slowly.
- However Calcium Carbonate can be heated to produce CALCIUM OXIDE (QUICKLIME).

CALCIUM CARBONATE ——— HEAT ——→ CALCIUM OXIDE + CARBON DIOXIDE
(limestone)   (quicklime)

- This can then be 'SLAKED' with water to produce CALCIUM HYDROXIDE (SLAKED LIME).

CALCIUM OXIDE ——— WATER ——→ CALCIUM HYDROXIDE
(quicklime)   (slaked lime)

- This, being a HYDROXIDE is quite strongly ALKALINE ...
  - ... and so can neutralise soils and lakes ...
    - ... much faster than just using ...
      - ... powdered limestone.

2. BUILDING MATERIAL

- Can be QUARRIED and cut ...
  - ... into BLOCKS and used directly ...
    - ... to build WALLS of houses ...
      - ... in regions where it is plentiful!
        - It is badly affected by ACID RAIN ...
          - ... but this takes a long time.

3. GLASS MAKING

- Glass is made by mixing ...
  - ... LIMESTONE, SAND and ...
    - ... SODA (sodium carbonate) ...
      - ... and heating the mixture until it melts.
        - When cool it is TRANSPARENT.

LIMESTONE + SAND + SODA ——HEAT——→ GLASS

4. CEMENT MAKING

- Powdered limestone and powdered CLAY ...
  - ... are roasted in a ROTARY KILN ...
    - ... to produce dry cement.
      - When the cement is mixed with WATER, SAND and GRAVEL (crushed rock) ...
        - ... a slow reaction takes place where ...
          - ... a HARD, STONE-LIKE BUILDING MATERIAL ...
            - ... called CONCRETE is produced.

CEMENT

- Limestone can be used as a neutralising agent, as a building material and for making glass and cement.
- Calcium carbonate ——HEAT——→ Calcium oxide + Carbon dioxide • Calcium oxide ——WATER——→ Calcium hydroxide

1. Fill in the spaces using the following words:
   HEAT, NON-POROUS, ORGANISMS, OXYGEN, FOSSIL FUEL, PLANKTON, MUD SEDIMENTS, PRESSURE.
   Crude oil was formed over millions of years from dead _____ mainly _____ which fell to the
   ocean floor and were covered by _____ . By the action of _____ and _____ in the
   absence of _____ , crude oil became trapped between _____ layers of sediment.
   Crude oil is a _____ .

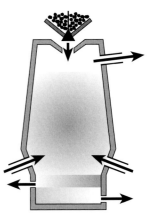

PETROLEUM GAS

A

NAPTHA

PARAFFIN

DIESEL OIL

FUEL OIL

B

2. The diagram opposite shows the different fractions of crude oil.
   a) Name the process that takes place to obtain the different fractions.
   b) Name the TWO fractions 'A' and 'B'.
   c) All the fractions contain TWO elements. Name these elements.

3. Fuel oil has a higher boiling point than paraffin.
   a) Which of these fuels is more viscous? Explain your answer.
   b) Which of these fuels is less volatile? Explain your answer.
   c) Which of these fuels is the more flammable? Explain your answer.

4. Very often the large chain molecules in crude oil are broken down into smaller chain molecules.
   a) What is the process called?
   b) Why are the smaller chain molecules more useful than the larger chain molecules?

5. A molecule of Methane has the following structure ...

   a) Draw the structure of (i) Ethane and (ii) Propane.
   b) Methane, Ethane and Propane are all 'saturated' hydrocarbons. Explain what this means.

6. a) What are Alkenes?
   b) Draw a diagram of the structure of a molecule of Ethene.
   c) Ethene can be polymerised to form which polymer?
   d) Explain why Ethane cannot be polymerised whereas Ethene can.

7. The diagram opposite shows a blast furnace used for the extraction of Iron.
   a) Which THREE substances are fed into the top of the furnace?
   b) What passes into the furnace via the tuyeres?
   c) Apart from Iron, what else is removed from the bottom of the furnace?

8. a) Explain why Aluminium cannot be extracted from its ore using the same process
   as for Iron.
   b) What is the name of the process used to extract Aluminium?
   c) In the extraction process which other product is also formed?

9. The equation below shows the reaction that takes place in the production of Ammonia.

   a) Name 'A' and 'B'.

   A + B ⇌ Ammonia

   b) Ammonia is used to make Ammonium Nitrate, a fertiliser (i) which acid is reacted with Ammonia to make
   Ammonium Nitrate? (ii) why is this an example of a neutralising reaction? (iii) what problems do nitrogen
   based fertilisers cause if they find their way into our water system?

10. The amount or percentage of Ammonia formed will change if the pressure and temperature is changed.
    a) Why is Ammonia produced at a pressure of 200 atmospheres and a temperature of 450°C?
    b) What happens to the percentage of Ammonia produced if this temperature is increased?
    Why is this an advantage and a disadvantage?
    c) What happens to the percentage of Ammonia produced if the pressure is increased?
    Why is this an advantage and a disadvantage?

11. Limestone has many uses. Name THREE uses.

Patterns of Behaviour

The 90 naturally occurring elements are grouped into 'FAMILIES' with SIMILAR PROPERTIES. These 'FAMILIES' of elements are then arranged into the PERIODIC TABLE.

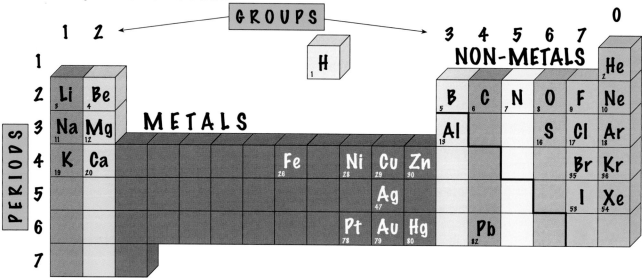

KEY POINTS

- The ELEMENTS are arranged in order of INCREASING PROTON NUMBER (see diagram).
- ELEMENTS in the SAME GROUP have the SAME NUMBER OF ELECTRONS IN THEIR OUTERMOST SHELL.
  This number also coincides with the GROUP NUMBER.
  Elements in the same group also have SIMILAR PROPERTIES.
- From left to right, ACROSS EACH PERIOD, A SHELL IS GRADUALLY FILLED WITH ELECTRONS ...
  ... in the next period, the next shell is filled etc (See P.9 for Electron configuration).

EARLY ATTEMPTS TO CLASSIFY THE ELEMENTS

1864 JOHN NEWLANDS

- Newlands only knew of the EXISTENCE OF 63 ELEMENTS. Many were undiscovered.
  - He arranged the KNOWN ELEMENTS in order of RELATIVE ATOMIC MASS and ...
    - ... found SIMILARITIES among every EIGHTH ELEMENT IN THE SERIES ...
      - ... Li Be B C N O F Na Mg Al ...
        - This makes sense, since the Noble gases (Group 0) weren't discovered until 1894.
          - In other words he noticed PERIODICITY ...
            - ... although the 'missing' elements caused problems.

1869 DIMITRI MENDELEEV

- Mendeleev realised that SOME ELEMENTS HAD YET TO BE DISCOVERED ...
  - ... so he left gaps to accommodate their eventual discovery.
    - He used his PERIODIC TABLE to PREDICT THE EXISTENCE OF OTHER ELEMENTS.

MODERN CHEMISTRY

- The discovery of ELECTRON CONFIGURATIONS gives us a sounder base for the table ...
  - ... since the key to SIMILARITIES amongst elements is ...
    - ... the NUMBER OF ELECTRONS IN THE OUTERMOST SHELL.
      - Group 1 elements have 1 electron in their outermost shell.
        - Group 2 elements have 2 electrons and so on.
          - Also, the Periodic table is now arranged in order of PROTON NUMBER.

- The periodic table is a list of elements arranged in order of increasing proton number. • Elements in the same group have the same number of electrons in their outermost shell. • The earliest attempts to classify the elements were by John Newlands, who arranged the known elements in order of relative atomic mass, and Dimitri Mendeleev who realised that some elements were yet to be discovered and he consequently left gaps for these elements.

GROUP 1 – The Alkali Metals

There are ⎡SIX METALS⎤ in this group ...
- ... but the top three in the group ...
- ... are the ones we need to deal with, ...
- ... especially SODIUM, Na and POTASSIUM, K.

The ⎡ALKALI METALS⎤ ...

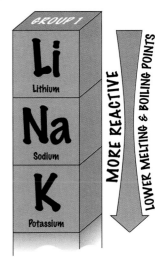

... ⎡REACT WITH NON-METALS TO FORM IONIC COMPOUNDS.⎤

- The metal atom LOSES ONE ELECTRON to form a 1^+ ION (a charged particle).

e.g.
Sodium   +   Chlorine   ⟶   Sodium Chloride
$$2Na_{(s)} \quad + \quad Cl_{2(g)} \quad \longrightarrow \quad 2NaCl_{(s)}$$

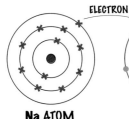

ELECTRON

Na ATOM
(1 electron in outer shell)

Cl ATOM
(7 electrons in outer shell)

Na⁺ ION

Cl⁻ ION

(Both ions have 8 electrons in outer shell)

> These positive and negative charges hold the molecule together in an IONIC BOND (See P.12).

... ⎡REACT WITH WATER RELEASING HYDROGEN.⎤

e.g.
Potassium   +   Water ⟶ Potassium Hydroxide   +   Hydrogen
$$2K_{(s)} \quad + \quad 2H_2O_{(l)} \quad \longrightarrow \quad 2KOH_{(aq)} \quad + \quad H_{2(g)}$$

As we move down this group the ALKALI METALS BECOME ⎡MORE REACTIVE⎤ ...
... and so they react more VIGOROUSLY with water ...
... they float, may melt ... and the hydrogen gas may ignite!!
Lithium reacts gently, Sodium more aggressively ...
... and Potassium so aggressively it melts and catches fire!!

> THE HYDROXIDES PRODUCED DISSOLVE IN WATER TO FORM ALKALINE SOLUTIONS. THIS IS WHY THEY'RE CALLED THE ALKALI METALS.

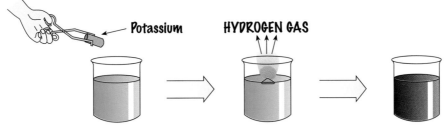

Potassium

HYDROGEN GAS

Beaker contains Water + Universal Indicator (green colour indicates water is neutral).

Beaker now contains Potassium Hydroxide dissolved in the water i.e. $KOH_{(aq)}$ (purple colour indicates an alkaline solution).

... ⎡HAVE LOWER MELTING AND BOILING POINTS AS WE GO DOWN THE GROUP.⎤

- The elements of group 1 are known as the alkali metals.
- They react with non-metals to form ionic compounds and with water releasing hydrogen.
- As we go down group 1 the elements have lower melting and boiling points, and become more reactive.

GROUP 7 – The Halogens

There are FIVE NON-METALS in this group ...

- ... but the top four in the group ...
- ... are the ones we need to be concerned about.

The HALOGENS ...

... ALL HAVE COLOURED VAPOURS.

Which in the case of chlorine and bromine are extremely pungent.

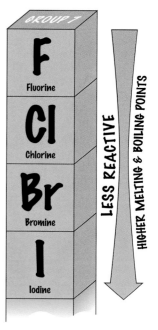

... EXIST AS MOLECULES MADE UP OF PAIRS OF ATOMS.

e.g. F_2, Cl_2, Br_2, I_2.

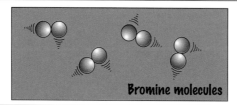

Bromine molecules

... REACT WITH METALS TO FORM IONIC SALTS.

The halogen atom GAINS ONE ELECTRON to form a 1^- ION (HALIDE ION).

e.g.　　Calcium　　＋　　Chlorine　　⟶　　Calcium Chloride
　　　　$Ca_{(s)}$　　＋　　$Cl_{2(g)}$　　⟶　　$CaCl_{2(s)}$

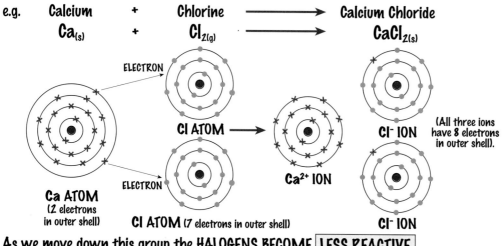

ELECTRON

Cl ATOM ⟶ Ca²⁺ ION

Ca ATOM
(2 electrons in outer shell)

ELECTRON

Cl ATOM (7 electrons in outer shell)

Cl⁻ ION

Cl⁻ ION

(All three ions have 8 electrons in outer shell).

These positive and negative charges hold the molecule together in an **IONIC BOND** (See P.12)

As we move down this group the HALOGENS BECOME LESS REACTIVE.

... CAN FORM COMPOUNDS WITH OTHER NON-METALLIC ELEMENTS.

e.g.　　Chlorine　　＋　　Hydrogen　　⟶　　Hydrogen Chloride
　　　　$Cl_{2(g)}$　　＋　　$H_{2(g)}$　　⟶　　$2HCl_{(g)}$

... CAN DISPLACE LESS REACTIVE HALOGENS FROM AQUEOUS SOLUTIONS OF THEIR SALTS.

CHLORINE will DISPLACE BOTH BROMINE and IODINE, BROMINE will DISPLACE IODINE.

e.g.　　Potassium Iodide　　＋　　Chlorine　　⟶　　Potassium Chloride　　＋　　Iodine
　　　　$2KI_{(aq)}$　　＋　　$Cl_{2(g)}$　　⟶　　$2KCl_{(aq)}$　　＋　　$I_{2(aq)}$

... HAVE HIGHER MELTING AND BOILING POINTS AS WE GO DOWN THE GROUP.

- The elements of group 7 are known as the halogens. • They all have coloured vapours, exist as molecules made up of a pair of atoms, react with metals to form ionic salts and can form compounds with other non-metallic compounds.
- As we go down Group 7 the elements have higher melting and boiling points, and become less reactive.

GROUP 0 – The Noble Gases (sometimes called Group 8)

There are │ SIX GASES │ in this group.

The │ NOBLE GASES │ ...

... │ EXIST AS INDIVIDUAL ATOMS (MONATOMIC). │

e.g. He, Ar, Kr etc rather than in pairs (DIATOMIC) ...
... like other gaseous elements (Cl_2, H_2 etc).

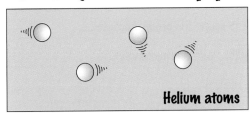

Helium atoms

... │ ARE CHEMICALLY UNREACTIVE. │

Because of this they are used as INERT gases ...
... in FILAMENT LAMPS and ELECTRICAL DISCHARGE TUBES.

Argon →

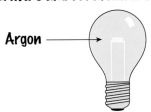

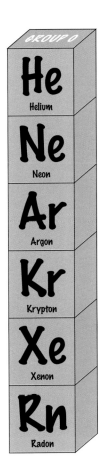

GROUP 0

He
Helium

Ne
Neon

Ar
Argon

Kr
Krypton

Xe
Xenon

Rn
Radon

THE TRANSITION METALS

If we look at the periodic table, we can see a middle section without group numbers ...

... These elements form the
TRANSITION METALS.

1	2						Fe		Ni	Cu	Zn	3	4	5	6	7	0
										Ag							
									Pt	Au	Hg						

We've just listed some of the common ones -
check their names on the periodic table (see P.64).

All you need to know is that the │ TRANSITION METALS │ ...

... │ HAVE HIGH MELTING POINTS. │ e.g. Gold has a melting point above 1000°C.

... │ CAN OFTEN BE USED AS CATALYSTS. │ e.g. Iron is used in the manufacture of ammonia.

... │ FORM COLOURED COMPOUNDS. │ e.g. Copper Sulphate is blue.

- The elements of Group 0 are known as the Noble gases.
- They exist as individual atoms and are chemically unreactive.
- The transition metals have high melting points, can often be used as catalysts and form coloured compounds.

EXPLANATION OF THE TRENDS WITHIN GROUP 1

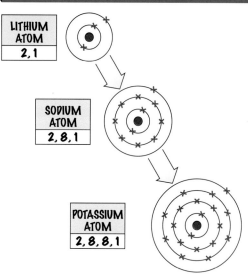

LITHIUM ATOM 2,1

SODIUM ATOM 2,8,1

POTASSIUM ATOM 2,8,8,1

They all have ...

- ... SIMILAR PROPERTIES ... because they have ...
- ... the SAME NUMBER OF ELECTRONS (ONE) IN THEIR OUTER SHELL ...
- ... i.e. the HIGHEST OCCUPIED ENERGY LEVEL CONTAINS ONE ELECTRON.

They become ...

- ... MORE REACTIVE as we go down the group, because ...
- ... the OUTER ELECTRON SHELL gets further away ...
- ... from the influence of the nucleus ...
- ... and so the electrons are MORE EASILY LOST.

EXPLANATION OF THE TRENDS WITHIN GROUP 7

FLUORINE ATOM 2,7

CHLORINE ATOM 2,8,7

They all have ...

- ... SIMILAR PROPERTIES ... because they have ...
- ... the SAME NUMBER OF ELECTRONS (SEVEN) IN THEIR OUTER SHELL ...
- ... i.e. the HIGHEST OCCUPIED ENERGY LEVEL CONTAINS SEVEN ELECTRONS.

They become ...

- ... LESS REACTIVE as we go down the group, because ...
- ... the OUTER ELECTRON SHELL gets further away ...
- ... from the influence of the nucleus ...
- ... and so electrons are LESS EASILY GAINED.

EXPLANATION OF THE TRENDS WITHIN GROUP 0

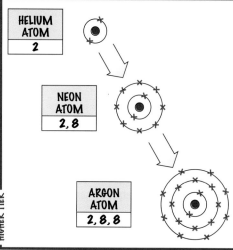

HELIUM ATOM 2

NEON ATOM 2,8

ARGON ATOM 2,8,8

They all have ...

- ... SIMILAR PROPERTIES ... because they have ...
- ... 'FULLY OCCUPIED' OUTER SHELLS (outer shells are full) ...
- ... i.e. the HIGHEST OCCUPIED ENERGY LEVEL IS FULL.

This means that ...

- ... they tend NOT TO WANT TO GAIN, LOSE OR SHARE ELECTRONS ...
- ... and therefore they are UNREACTIVE and MONATOMIC.

- Elements in a particular group all have similar properties since they all have the same number of electrons in their outer shell. • Group 1 elements become more reactive as we go down the group.
- Group 7 elements become less reactive as we go down the group.
- Group 0 elements are all unreactive and monatomic

HIGHER TIER

METALS AND NON-METALS IN THE PERIODIC TABLE

As we have seen, the PERIODIC TABLE ...
... arranges ALL THE ELEMENTS ...
... in order of INCREASING PROTON NUMBER.
It's just a way of CLASSIFYING the elements.

> MORE THAN THREE QUARTERS OF THE ELEMENTS ARE METALS.

> LESS THAN ONE QUARTER OF THE ELEMENTS ARE NON-METALS.

NON-METALS

METALS

COMPARING METALS AND NON-METALS

METALS	NON - METALS
• All are SOLIDS at room temperature (except Mercury which is a liquid.)	• Half of them are GASES, and Bromine is a LIQUID at room temperature.
• Have HIGH MELTING POINTS	• Have LOW MELTING POINTS and BOILING POINTS
• Are SHINY at least when freshly cut	• Are mostly DULL
• Can be HAMMERED and BENT into shape. Usually, tough and strong.	• Usually BRITTLE and CRUMBLE easily when solid.
• GOOD CONDUCTORS of heat and electricity when solid or liquid.	• POOR CONDUCTORS of heat and electricity when solid or liquid.
• Form ALLOYS (mixtures of metals)	• Don't (obviously!) form alloys.

HOW THESE PROPERTIES ARE PUT TO GOOD USE IN THREE COMMON METALS

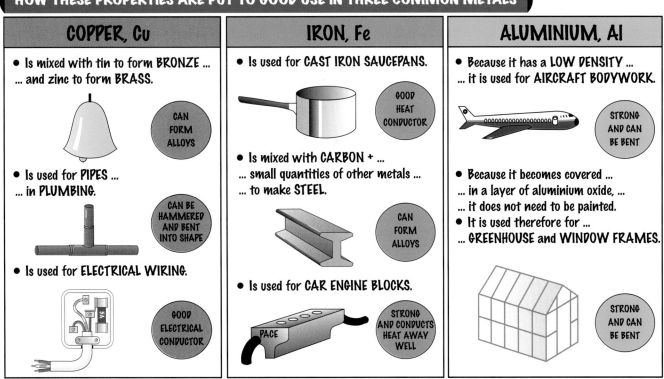

COPPER, Cu

• Is mixed with tin to form BRONZE ...
... and zinc to form BRASS.

CAN FORM ALLOYS

• Is used for PIPES ...
... in PLUMBING.

CAN BE HAMMERED AND BENT INTO SHAPE

• Is used for ELECTRICAL WIRING.

GOOD ELECTRICAL CONDUCTOR

IRON, Fe

• Is used for CAST IRON SAUCEPANS.

GOOD HEAT CONDUCTOR

• Is mixed with CARBON + ...
... small quantities of other metals ...
... to make STEEL.

CAN FORM ALLOYS

• Is used for CAR ENGINE BLOCKS.

STRONG AND CONDUCTS HEAT AWAY WELL

ALUMINIUM, Al

• Because it has a LOW DENSITY ...
... it is used for AIRCRAFT BODYWORK.

STRONG AND CAN BE BENT

• Because it becomes covered ...
... in a layer of aluminium oxide, ...
... it does not need to be painted.
• It is used therefore for ...
... GREENHOUSE and WINDOW FRAMES.

STRONG AND CAN BE BENT

• More than three quarters of the elements in the periodic table are metals, the others are non-metals.
• Different metals have different uses because of the properties they have.

By observing how metals react with OXYGEN (air), WATER, and DILUTE ACID, we can place them in order of how REACTIVE they are. This is called the REACTIVITY SERIES.

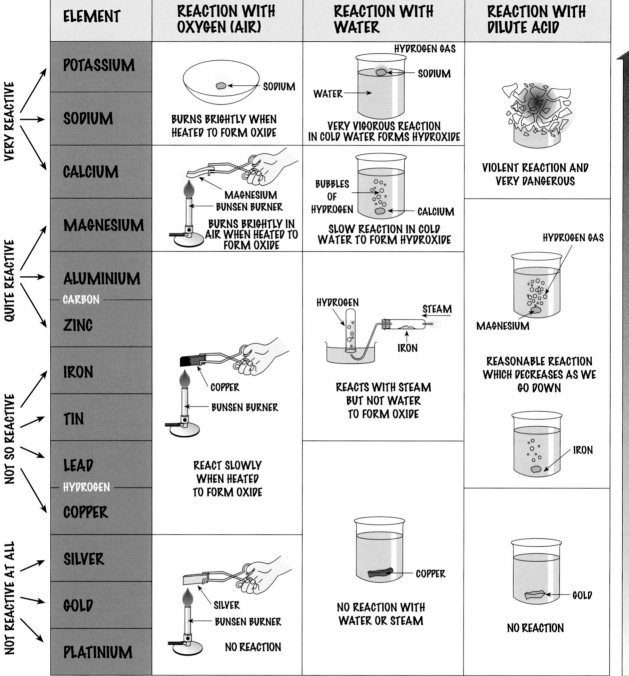

INCREASING REACTIVITY

ELEMENT	REACTION WITH OXYGEN (AIR)	REACTION WITH WATER	REACTION WITH DILUTE ACID
POTASSIUM			
SODIUM			
CALCIUM			
MAGNESIUM			
ALUMINIUM			
CARBON			
ZINC			
IRON			
TIN			
LEAD			
HYDROGEN			
COPPER			
SILVER			
GOLD			
PLATINIUM			

VERY REACTIVE
QUITE REACTIVE
NOT SO REACTIVE
NOT REACTIVE AT ALL

REACTION WITH AIR Nearly all the metals react with OXYGEN to form OXIDES.

METAL + OXYGEN ⟶ METAL OXIDES.

REACTION WITH WATER Some metals react to produce HYDROXIDES (or OXIDES) and HYDROGEN.

METAL + WATER ⟶ METAL HYDROXIDE (or OXIDE) + HYDROGEN

REACTION WITH DILUTE ACIDS Many metals react with acids ...

... to produce a SALT and HYDROGEN.

METAL + ACID ⟶ METAL SALT + HYDROGEN

HYDROGEN POP!!! LIGHTED SPLINT

TEST FOR HYDROGEN

• The Hydrogen given off in these reactions can be identified in the following way ...

• The reactivity series lists metals in order of their reactivity based on their reactions with oxygen (air), water and dilute acid.

A DISPLACEMENT REACTION is one in which a MORE REACTIVE metal displaces a LESS REACTIVE metal from a compound in a chemical reaction.

There's just one "incredibly important rule" to remember!

> **IF THE PURE METAL IS HIGHER IN THE REACTIVITY SERIES THAN THE METAL IN THE COMPOUND, THEN DISPLACEMENT WILL HAPPEN.**

Let's consider what happens when an IRON NAIL is put into a beaker of COPPER SULPHATE SOLUTION.

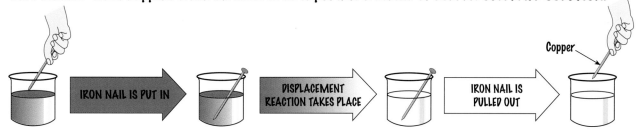

If we look at the POSITIONS of IRON and COPPER in the REACTIVITY SERIES, then what's gone on above can easily be explained

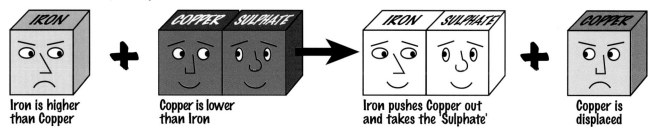

Iron is higher than Copper

Copper is lower than Iron

Iron pushes Copper out and takes the 'Sulphate'

Copper is displaced

This is why an iron nail becomes coated with Copper when it's put in Copper Sulphate Solution, and why the blue solution becomes clear Iron Sulphate solution.

SOME MORE EXAMPLES OF DISPLACEMENT

Example No. 1
ZINC + COPPER SULPHATE SOLUTION
Remember the "Rule". Which is HIGHER in the Reactivity series?

ZINC + COPPER SULPHATE ⟶ ZINC SULPHATE + COPPER

Yes! Zinc is higher so it displaces the copper forming Zinc Sulphate.

Example No. 2
COPPER + LEAD NITRATE SOLUTION
Remember the "Rule". Which is HIGHER in the Reactivity series?

COPPER + LEAD NITRATE ⟶ LEAD NITRATE + COPPER

No! Copper is lower in the series than Lead so no reaction takes place.

SUMMING UP

- Look at the Reactivity Series ...
- ... If the pure metal is higher than the metal in the metal compound ...
- ... then simply swop the metals around!!
- If it isn't there's no reaction.

- If a pure metal is higher in the reactivity series than the metal in the compound then a displacement reaction will happen.
- If the pure metal is lower then no displacement reaction takes place.

Compounds of alkali metals and halogens have very different properties than the elements from which they are made. The use we make of these compounds depends on these different properties.

INDUSTRIAL ELECTROLYSIS OF SODIUM CHLORIDE SOLUTION (BRINE)

Sodium Chloride (common salt) is a compound of an ALKALI METAL and a HALOGEN.
It is found in large quantities in the sea and in underground deposits.
Electrolysis of sodium chloride solution produces ...

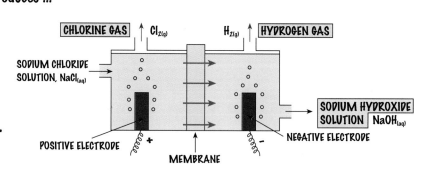

- CHLORINE GAS ...

  ... at the POSITIVE ELECTRODE.

- HYDROGEN GAS ...

  ... at the NEGATIVE ELECTRODE.

- SODIUM HYDROXIDE SOLUTION ...

  ... which is passed out of the cell.

HOW THE PRODUCTS ARE USED

The products of the electrolysis of sodium chloride have many uses:

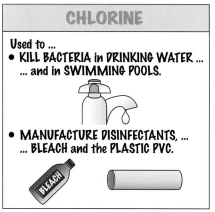

CHLORINE

Used to ...
- KILL BACTERIA in DRINKING WATER ... ... and in SWIMMING POOLS.

- MANUFACTURE DISINFECTANTS, ... BLEACH and the PLASTIC PVC.

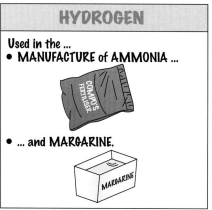

HYDROGEN

Used in the ...
- MANUFACTURE of AMMONIA ...

- ... and MARGARINE.

SODIUM HYDROXIDE

Used in the ...
- MANUFACTURE of SOAP, ...

- ... PAPER, ...

- ... and CERAMICS.

You also need to know the laboratory test for Chlorine, which is ...
... that it BLEACHES DAMP LITMUS PAPER (i.e. removes the colour).

SILVER HALIDES

The main use of these HALIDES is in the making of PHOTOGRAPHIC FILM and PHOTOGRAPHIC PAPER.

SILVER CHLORIDE,
SILVER BROMIDE
and SILVER IODIDE ...

... are REDUCED by LIGHT , X-RAYS

and RADIATION from RADIOACTIVE SUBSTANCES ☢ to ...

... SILVER

THIS IS PRECIPITATED
TO FORM A PHOTOGRAPHIC
IMAGE.

HYDROGEN HALIDES

These are all GASES which dissolve in water to produce ACIDIC SOLUTIONS e.g. HF (Hydrogen Fluoride),
HCl (Hydrogen Chloride). $HCl_{(g)}$ ⟶

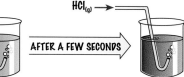

Beaker contains WATER
and UNIVERSAL
INDICATOR (green colour
indicates water is neutral).

AFTER A FEW SECONDS

$HCl_{(g)}$ ⟶

Beaker now contains
HYDROGEN CHLORIDE
DISSOLVED IN WATER,
$HCl_{(aq)}$ (red colour indicates
an acidic solution).

- Industrial electrolysis of sodium chloride solution (brine) produces chlorine gas, hydrogen gas and sodium hydroxide solution. • Silver halides are reduced by light, X-rays and radiation to silver. • Hydrogen halides are gases which dissolve in water to produce acidic solutions.

INDICATORS

These are really useful dyes which CHANGE COLOUR ...

- ... depending on whether they're in ACIDIC or ALKALINE solutions.
- Some are just simple substances such as LITMUS which changes from RED to BLUE or vice versa ...
- ... whereas others are mixtures of dyes such as UNIVERSAL INDICATOR which ..
- ... show a RANGE OF COLOUR to indicate just how ACIDIC or ALKALINE a substance is.

THE pH SCALE

This measures the ACIDITY, ALKALINITY, or NEUTRALITY of a solution ...

... ACROSS A 14 POINT SCALE

VERY ACIDIC					SLIGHTLY ACIDIC	NEUTRAL	SLIGHTLY ALKALINE						VERY ALKALINE
1	2	3	4	5	6	7	8	9	10	11	12	13	14

When used with UNIVERSAL INDICATOR, we get the following range of colours:-

e.g. Battery Acid / Stomach Acid | Lemon Juice / Vinegar | Soda Water | Water | Soap | Baking Powder | Washing Soda | Oven Cleaner | Potassium Hydroxide

NEUTRALISATION

Basically, this occurs when the right amounts of acid and alkali react ...
... to "cancel" each other out to form a salt and water (which is NEUTRAL).

| ACID | + | ALKALI | ⟶ | SALT | + | WATER |

e.g.

| HCl | + | KOH | ⟶ | KCl | + | H_2O |

HYDROCHLORIC ACID STRONG ACID, pH 1 | POTASSIUM HYDROXIDE STRONG ALKALI, pH 14 | POTASSIUM CHLORIDE | WATER NEUTRAL, pH 7

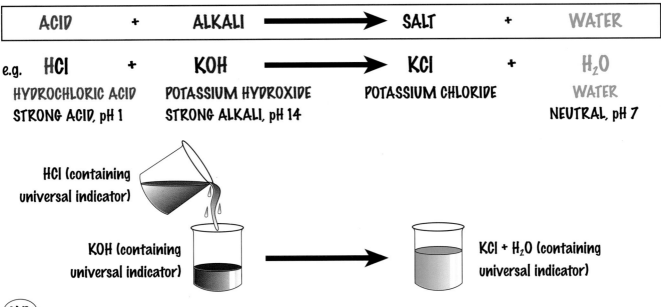

HCl (containing universal indicator)

KOH (containing universal indicator)

KCl + H_2O (containing universal indicator)

(N.B.)

The demonstration above will only work if ...
... BOTH BEAKERS CONTAIN THE SAME NUMBER ...
... OF ACID AND ALKALI MOLECULES, SO THAT THEY NEUTRALISE EACH OTHER EXACTLY.

- Indicators change colour depending on whether they are in acidic or alkaline solutions.
- The pH scale measures the acidity, alkalinity or neutrality of a solution.
- Acid + Alkali ⟶ Salt + Water

COMMON ACIDS AND ALKALIS

As we have seen an **ACID** reacts with an **ALKALI** to produce a **SALT** and WATER. The particular salt produced depends on ...
- ... the METAL in the ALKALI ...
- ... and the ACID USED.

- The three most common acids you will come across are ...

HYDROCHLORIC ACID   SULPHURIC ACID   NITRIC ACID

- ... and the three most common alkalis you will come across are.

SODIUM HYDROXIDE   POTASSIUM HYDROXIDE   CALCIUM HYDROXIDE

What we get when we react one the acids above with one of the alkalis can best be summarised in a table.

	HYDROCHLORIC ACID	SULPHURIC ACID	NITRIC ACID
+ SODIUM HYDROXIDE	→ SODIUM CHLORIDE + WATER	→ SODIUM SULPHATE + WATER	→ SODIUM NITRATE + WATER
+ POTASSIUM HYDROXIDE	→ POTASSIUM CHLORIDE + WATER	→ POTASSIUM SULPHATE + WATER	→ POTASSIUM NITRATE + WATER
+ CALCIUM HYDROXIDE	→ CALCIUM CHLORIDE + WATER	→ CALCIUM SULPHATE + WATER	→ CALCIUM NITRATE + WATER

You will have noticed that neutralising ...
- HYDROCHLORIC ACID produces <u>CHLORIDE</u> salts.
- SULPHURIC ACID produces <u>SULPHATE</u> salts.
- NITRIC ACID produces <u>NITRATE</u> salts.

METAL OXIDES AND HYDROXIDES

The **ALKALIS** mentioned above are made by dissolving the METAL OXIDES or HYDROXIDES in WATER.

SODIUM
POTASSIUM ⟶ OXIDES or HYDROXIDES dissolve in water to form **ALKALIS.**
CALCIUM

Sodium Hydroxide

Water
(containing universal
indicator)   ON ADDING AND STIRRING   Sodium Hydroxide
solution
(an alkaline solution)

NON-METAL OXIDES

In contrast to the above, soluble OXIDES of NON-METALS produce acidic solutions:

CARBON DIOXIDE
SULPHUR DIOXIDE ⟶ dissolve in water to form **ACIDS.**
NITROGEN DIOXIDE

Carbon Dioxide ⟶
Water
(containing universal
indicator)   AFTER A FEW SECONDS   Carbon Dioxide ⟶   Carbon Dioxide has
dissolved in the water
to form an acidic
solution

- The particular salt produced when an acid reacts with an alkali depends on the metal in the alkali and the acid used.
- Metal oxides or hydroxides dissolved in water form alkaline solutions.
- Soluble oxides of non-metals dissolve in water producing acidic solutions.

Acids and Alkalis.

Universal indicator
Shows a range of
colours.

Indicators

Some are Litmus
which charge red/blue.

Useful dyes which
Change colour.
depending on what kind
of solution they are
placed in Acid/Alkali.

The PH Scale.

Very acidic — Slightly acidic — Neutral — Slightly Alkaline — Very Alkaline

←——————————→ 7 ←——————————→
1 2 3 4 5 6   7   8 9 10 11 12 13 14

dark red   orange Yellow   green   blue   dark blue   purple.

Neutralisation occurs when the right amounts
are reacted "cancel" each other out to form
Salt and Water (which is neutral)

Acid + Alkali ——→ Salt + water.

Summary questions   Patterns of behaviour.

(a) Li = Lithum   N=   Ca =   Fe = Iron K = Potassium
b) ~~K~~ i) H ii) Li   iii) S.

c i) zinc   copper Iron ii) Sodium, oxygen chlorine

2.

3.
a. ~~They both have one electron in the outer shell~~
They loose 1 electron and this
causes then to have a full   outer
shell of electrons and form a
charged petricle.
b. Na + H_2O → NaH_2O
~~Na~~ Sodium + water →   Sodium Oxide.
c. Transition metals have high melting
points
+ are coloured compounds.

1. The diagram below shows part of the Periodic Table.

										H								He
Li	Be											B	C	N	O	F	Ne
Na	Mg											Al	Si	P	S	Cl	Ar
K	Ca	Sc	Ti	V	Cr	Mn	Fe	Co	Ni	Cu	Zn	Ga	Ge	As	Se	Br	Kr

a) What is the name of the elements represented by the following symbols:
(i) Li (ii) N (iii) Ca (iv) Fe (v) K.
b) Which element from the Periodic Table above has (i) the lowest proton number? (ii) the highest proton number? (iii) has a proton number of 16? (Think about this before looking at the Periodic Table!!)
c) Give the name and symbol of THREE elements that are: (i) metals (ii) non-metals.

2. Explain the work of John Newlands and Dimitri Mendeleev in their attempt to classify the elements.

3. Lithium, Sodium and Potassium are the first three elements in Group 1 of the Periodic Table.
a) Explain why these elements form 1⁺IONS when they react with non-metals.
b) A piece of Sodium is added to water. A reaction takes place where a solution of Sodium Hydroxide and an unknown colourless gas are formed.
(i) What is the name of this unknown gas?
(ii) If Universal Indicator was present in the water, explain using diagrams what would happen to the colour of the water when the Sodium was added.
c) A piece of Potassium is added to water. Would you get a more vigorous or less vigorous reaction?
Explain your answer.

4. Chlorine, Bromine and Iodine are three elements in Group 7 of the Periodic Table.
a) Explain why these elements form 1⁻IONS when they react with metals?
b) The table below gives the melting and boiling points of Chlorine, Bromine and Iodine in no particular order.
Which element corresponds to 'X', 'Y' and 'Z'?

	X	Y	Z
MELTING POINT	114°C	-101°C	-7°C
BOILING POINT	184°C	-35°C	59°C

5. Helium, Neon and Argon are the first three elements in Group 0.
a) What are these gases better known as?
b) Write down the name of TWO other gases from this group?
c) Explain why Argon is a suitable gas for use in a filament lamp.

6. a) Name SIX Transition Metals.
b) Which Transition Metal (i) has the symbol Hg? (ii) is used as a catalyst in the production of Nitric Acid?

7. Explain why:
a) Elements in Group 1 have similar properties and their reactivity _increases_ as we go down the group.
b) Elements in Group 7 have similar properties and the reactivity _decreases_ as we go down the group.
c) Elements in Group 0 have similar properties and are unreactive.

8. This question is about THREE metals: Copper, Iron and Aluminium. Which is used to make ...
a) Steel?
b) Window frames?
c) Car engine blocks?
d) Pipes for plumbing?

9. Below are the results of some experiments carried out on four different metals.

METAL	Reaction with Air	Reaction with Water	Reaction with Dilute Acid
A	Burns brightly	Slow reaction	Reasonable reaction with many bubbles of gas produced
B	No reaction	No reaction	Slow reaction with a few bubbles of gas produced
C	No reaction	No reaction	No reaction
D	Burns violently	Very vigorous reaction	Violent reaction

a) Using the results above list the FOUR metals 'A', 'B' 'C' and 'D' in order of reactivity with the most reactive first.
b) The reaction of 'A' with dilute acid produces a gas (i) name the gas (ii) describe a simple laboratory test for this gas.

10. a) Explain using diagrams why an iron nail becomes coated with Copper when it is put into a solution of Copper Sulphate.
b) What would happen if a gold ring was put into a solution of Copper Sulphate? Explain your answer.

11. Chlorine, Hydrogen and Sodium Hydroxide are all made by the electrolysis of Sodium Chloride solution. The diagram below shows the electrolysis cell used.
a) Name 'A', 'B' and 'C'.
b) The products all have their particular uses.
Which product is used in the manufacture of
(i) margarine? (ii) disinfectants? (iii) fertilisers? (iv) soap?

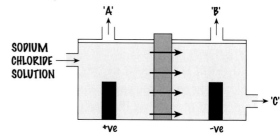

12. The beaker below (1) contains water with a few drops of Universal Indicator added to it.

a) What colour would the water become? Explain your answer.
b) Some Hydrogen Fluoride gas is passed into the water as shown above (2).
(i) What colour would the water become? (ii) Explain your answer.

13. a) What colour would (i) lemon juice (ii) washing soda and (iii) soda water turn Universal Indicator?
b) Copy and complete the following equation.

Acid + Alkali ⟶ ▢

Which ONE of the following would produce (i) a neutral (ii) an acidic and (iii) an alkali solution.
All solutions are the same strength!
A) 100cm³ of Hydrochloric acid is added to 90cm³ of Sodium Hydroxide.
B) 100cm³ of Hydrochloric acid is added to 100cm³ of Sodium Hydroxide.
C) 100cm³ of Hydrochloric acid is added to 110cm³ of Sodium Hydroxide. Explain your answers.

14. Copy and complete the following word equations.
a) Sulphuric Acid + Calcium Hydroxide ⟶
b) Nitric Acid + Sodium Hydroxide ⟶
c) Hydrochloric Acid + Potassium Hydroxide ⟶

15. A beaker contains water. Explain what would happen to the pH of the water if Sodium Hydroxide is added to the water.

16. A beaker contains water. Explain what would happen to the pH of the water if Sulphur Dioxide was passed into the water.

Chemical Reactions

USING CHEMICAL SYMBOLS

- Each element is represented by a different symbol ...
  ... e.g. Fe for Iron, Na for Sodium, C for Carbon, and O for Oxygen.
- These symbols are all contained in the PERIODIC TABLE on page 64.
- These symbols can be used to represent molecules of compounds and can show us the RATIO OF ATOMS FROM DIFFERENT ELEMENTS which are combined to form the compounds. These are chemical formulae e.g. ...

$$H_2O$$

This is water, and the formula tells us that it consists of 2 atoms of Hydrogen and 1 atom of oxygen.

$$CH_4$$

This is methane, and the formula tells us that it consists of 1 atom of Carbon and 4 atoms of Hydrogen.

$$NaOH$$

This is Sodium Hydroxide, and the formula tells us that it consists of 1 atom of Sodium, 1 atom of oxygen and 1 atom of Hydrogen.

USING THESE SYMBOLS and STATE SYMBOLS IN CHEMICAL EQUATIONS

Chemical reactions can be represented using chemical formulae for the REACTANTS and PRODUCTS. e.g ...
The word equation ...

SODIUM + WATER ⟶ SODIUM HYDROXIDE + HYDROGEN

Reactants   Products

... can be represented by the formulae and symbol equation ...

$$Na_{(s)} + H_2O_{(l)} \longrightarrow NaOH_{(aq)} + H_{2(g)}$$

... This means that ...

Sodium which and **Water which** produce **Sodium hydroxide** and **Hydrogen**
  is solid   is liquid   in aqueous solution   which is a gas

- (s), (l), (aq) and (g) are known as the STATE SYMBOLS.

WHAT YOU REALLY NEED TO KNOW

For the tier of the syllabus for which you are entered, you need to be able ...
- ... to write WORD EQUATIONS for ALL reactions referred to in your tier ...
- ... to recall the FORMULAE of ALL SIMPLE COVALENT COMPOUNDS referred to in your tier, ...
- ... to write down the correct FORMULAE for SIMPLE IONIC COMPOUNDS, ...
- ... to interpret CHEMICAL FORMULAE or SYMBOLIC REPRESENTATIONS of molecules, ...
- ... to interpret supplied SYMBOL EQUATIONS including STATE SYMBOLS.

SIMPLE COVALENT FORMULAE	
Water H_2O	Nitrogen N_2
Carbon dioxide CO_2	Sulphur dioxide SO_2
Ammonia NH_3	
Hydrogen H_2	
Oxygen O_2	

SIMPLE IONIC FORMULAE	
Sodium chloride $NaCl$	Sodium hydroxide $NaOH$
Calcium chloride $CaCl_2$	Potassium hydroxide KOH
Magnesium oxide MgO	Calcium hydroxide $Ca(OH)_2$
Hydrochloric acid HCl	Calcium carbonate $CaCO_3$
Sulphuric acid H_2SO_4	Aluminium oxide Al_2O_3
Nitric acid HNO_3	Iron oxide Fe_2O_3

- All elements are represented by a different symbol.
- Any chemical reaction can be represented using chemical formulae for the reactants and the products.

SOME IMPORTANT PRINCIPLES

- The TOTAL MASS of the PRODUCT(S) of a chemical reaction is ALWAYS ...
  ... EXACTLY EQUAL to the TOTAL MASS of the REACTANT(S).
  (This is because the products of a chemical reaction are made up from exactly the same atoms as the reactants!!.)
- Symbol chemical equations must, therefore, always be balanced. In other words ...

> THERE MUST BE THE SAME NUMBER OF ATOMS OF EACH ELEMENT ON THE REACTANT SIDE OF THE EQUATION AS THERE IS ON THE PRODUCT SIDE OF THE EQUATION.

BALANCING EQUATIONS   There are FOUR IMPORTANT STEPS ...

STEP 1: WRITE A WORD EQUATION FOR THE CHEMICAL REACTION.
STEP 2: SUBSTITUTE IN FORMULAE FOR THE ELEMENTS OR COMPOUNDS INVOLVED.
STEP 3: BALANCE THE EQUATION BY ADDING NUMBERS IN FRONT OF THE REACTANTS AND/OR PRODUCTS.
STEP 4: WRITE DOWN A BALANCED SYMBOL EQUATION (INCLUDING STATE SYMBOLS - see previous page).

EXAMPLE 1 ... The reaction of Calcium with Oxygen.

STEP 1: CALCIUM   +   OXYGEN ⟶ CALCIUM OXIDE

STEP 2: Ca + O_2 ⟶ CaO

STEP 3:   'REACTANTS'   'PRODUCT'

(Ca)   +   (O)(O) ⟶ (Ca)(O)

But now, there's only one O on the 'product side', so we must add another CaO ...

(Ca)   +   (O)(O) ⟶ (Ca)(O) (Ca)(O)

But now, there's only one Ca on the 'reactant side', so we must add another Ca ...

(Ca)(Ca)   +   (O)(O) ⟶ (Ca)(O) (Ca)(O)

There are two Calcium atoms and two Oxygen atoms on each side - IT'S BALANCED!!

STEP 4: $2Ca_{(s)}$ + $O_{2(g)}$ ⟶ $2CaO_{(s)}$

EXAMPLE 2 ... The production of Ammonia.

STEP 1: NITROGEN   +   HYDROGEN ⟶ AMMONIA

STEP 2: N_2 + H_2 ⟶ NH_3

STEP 3:   'REACTANTS'   'PRODUCT'

(N)(N)   +   (H)(H) ⟶ (N)(H)(H)(H)

But now, there's only one N on the 'product side', so we must add another NH₃ ...

(N)(N)   +   (H)(H) ⟶ (N)(H)(H)(H) (N)(H)(H)(H)

But now, there are only two H's on the 'reactant side', so we must add two more H₂ ...

(N)(N)   +   (H)(H)(H)(H)(H)(H) ⟶ (N)(H)(H)(H) (N)(H)(H)(H)

There are two Nitrogen atoms and six Hydrogen atoms on each side - IT'S BALANCED!!

STEP 4: $N_{2(g)}$ + $3H_{2(g)}$ ⟶ $2NH_{3(g)}$

- In all chemical reactions the total mass of the product(s) is always exactly equal to the total mass of the reactant(s).
- A balanced chemical equation will always have the same number of atoms of each element on the reactant side of the equation as on the product side of the equation.

RELATIVE ATOMIC MASS, A_r

Atoms are too small for their actual atomic mass to be of much use to us. To make things more manageable we use RELATIVE ATOMIC MASS, A_r.

- Basically this is just the MASS OF A PARTICULAR ATOM ...
- ... compared to the MASS OF AN ATOM OF HYDROGEN, (the lightest atom of all.)

(In fact we now use 1/12th the mass of a CARBON ATOM, but it doesn't make any real difference!)

If we look at the PERIODIC TABLE (P.64) We can see that all the elements have TWO NUMBERS ...

1 **H** 1	12 **C** 6	16 **O** 8	23 **Na** 11	24 **Mg** 12	32 **S** 16	35 **Cl** 17	39 **K** 19	40 **Ca** 20	63 **Cu** 29
HYDROGEN	CARBON	OXYGEN	SODIUM	MAGNESIUM	SULPHUR	CHLORINE	POTASSIUM	CALCIUM	COPPER

- The larger of the two numbers is the **MASS NUMBER** of the element (See P.8), but ...
- ... it also very conveniently doubles as the **RELATIVE ATOMIC MASS,** A_r of the element.
- So, in the examples above Carbon is twelve times heavier than Hydrogen, but ...
- ... is only half as heavy as Magnesium, which is three quarters as heavy as Sulphur ...
- ... which is twice as heavy as Oxygen and so on, and so on ...
- We can use this idea to calculate the RELATIVE FORMULA MASS of compounds.

RELATIVE FORMULA MASS, M_r

The relative formula mass of a compound is simply the relative atomic masses of all its elements added together. So in other words, if water has an M_r of 18, it is 18 times heavier than an atom of Hydrogen, or 1.5 times heavier than a Carbon atom! Get it?

- To calculate M_r, we need the FORMULA OF THE COMPOUND, and the A_r of ALL THE ATOMS INVOLVED.

EXAMPLE 1: Using the data above, find the M_r of Water, H_2O

STEP 1: the Formula ... H_2O

STEP 2: the A_r's ... $(2 \times 1) + 16$

STEP 3: the M_r ... $2 + 16 = \underline{18}$

EXAMPLE 2: Using the data above, find the M_r of Sodium Hydroxide, NaOH

STEP 1: the Formula ...   NaOH

STEP 2: the A_r's ... $23 + 16 + 1$

STEP 3: the M_r ... $23 + 16 + 1 = \underline{40}$

EXAMPLE 3: Using the data above, find the M_r of Potassium Carbonate, K_2CO_3

STEP 1: the Formula ... K_2CO_3

STEP 2: the A_r's ... $(39 \times 2) + 12 + (16 \times 3)$

STEP 3: the M_r ... $78 + 12 + 48 = \underline{138}$

- The relative atomic mass, A_r, of an atom is its mass compared to the mass of a hydrogen atom.
- The relative formula mass, M_r, of a compound is the relative atomic masses of all its elements added together.

WORKING OUT PERCENTAGES

If 12 pupils in a class of 30 are left handed, you could work out the percentage of left handers in the following way ...

$$\frac{\text{No. OF LEFT HANDERS}}{\text{TOTAL No. IN CLASS}} \times 100 \quad , \text{... in this case } \frac{12}{30} \times 100 = \underline{40.0\%}$$

You use exactly the same principle in calculating percentage mass of an element in a compound, except this time we express it as ...

$$\frac{\text{MASS OF ELEMENT IN THE COMPOUND}}{\text{RELATIVE FORMULA MASS OF COMPOUND (M}_r\text{)}} \times 100 \quad \text{The mass of the compound is the relative formula mass.}$$

- All you need to know is the FORMULA OF THE COMPOUND and the RELATIVE ATOMIC MASS of all the atoms.

EXAMPLES OF PERCENTAGE MASS QUESTIONS (See P.39 for data on A_r's of elements).

EXAMPLE 1 "Calculate the percentage mass of Magnesium in Magnesium Oxide, MgO."

MASS OF MAGNESIUM = 24 (since this is its A_r, and there's only one atom of it!).

RELATIVE FORMULA MASS (M_r) of MgO = (A_r for Mg) 24 + (A_r for O) 16 = 40.

Substituting into our formula ... $\dfrac{\text{MASS OF ELEMENT}}{M_r \text{ OF COMPOUND}} \times 100$, ... we get $\frac{24}{40} \times 100 = \underline{60.0\%}$

EXAMPLE 2 "Calculate the percentage mass of Oxygen in Magnesium Carbonate, $MgCO_3$."

MASS OF OXYGEN = $16 \times 3 = 48$ (since its A_r is 16 and there are three atoms of it!).

RELATIVE FORMULA MASS (M_r) of $MgCO_3$ = (A_r for Mg) 24 + (A_r for C) 12 + (A_r for O x 3) 48 = 84.

Substituting into our formula ... $\dfrac{\text{MASS OF ELEMENT}}{M_r \text{ OF COMPOUND}} \times 100$, ... we get $\frac{48}{84} \times 100 = \underline{57.1\%}$

EXAMPLE 3 "Calculate the percentage mass of Potassium in Potassium Carbonate, K_2CO_3."

MASS OF POTASSIUM = $39 \times 2 = 78$ (since its A_r is 39 and there are two atoms of it!).

RELATIVE FORMULA MASS (M_r) of K_2CO_3 = (A_r for K x 2) 78 + (A_r for C) 12 + (A_r for O x 3) 48 = 138.

Substituting into our formula ... $\dfrac{\text{MASS OF ELEMENT}}{M_r \text{ OF COMPOUND}} \times 100$, ... we get $\frac{78}{138} \times 100 = \underline{56.5\%}$

SUMMARY

All we're really doing is DIVIDING THE MASS OF THE ELEMENT ...
... by the MASS OF THE COMPOUND and multiplying by 100!

- Just make sure you account for **all** the atoms in the element or compound.

- The percentage mass of an element contained in a compound can be calculated by using:

$$\frac{\text{Mass of element in the compound}}{\text{Relative formula mass of compound (M}_r\text{)}} \times 100$$

HIGHER TIER

We sometimes need to be able to work out how much of a substance is USED or FORMED in a chemical reaction, when we are given certain data. To do this, we need to know:-

* ... the RELATIVE FORMULA MASS, M_r of the REACTANTS and PRODUCTS (or the A_r of all the elements.)

and, * the BALANCED SYMBOL EQUATION for the reaction concerned.

By substituting the first of these into the second we can work out ...

THE RATIO OF MASS OF REACTANT TO MASS OF PRODUCT

CALCULATING THE MASS OF A PRODUCT

❶ "What mass of Hydrogen is produced by the electrolysis of 4g of water?" A_r : H = 1, O = 16.

| STEP 1: | Write down the equation. | $2H_2O \longrightarrow 2H_2 + O_2$ (This would be given) |

| STEP 2: | Calculate M_r of relevant bits. | $2[(2 \times 1) + 16] \longrightarrow 2(2 \times 1)$ Ignore the oxygen. |

Since the question only mentions Hydrogen and water, we ignore anything else!

This is ... | THE RATIO OF MASS OF REACTANT ... | 36 $\longrightarrow$ 4 | ... TO MASS OF PRODUCT |

| STEP 3: | Apply this ratio to the question.

If 36 grams of water produces 4 grams of Hydrogen, ...

... then 1 gram of water produces $\frac{4}{36}$ grams of Hydrogen, ...

... and 4 grams of water produces $\frac{4}{36}$ x 4 = <u>0.44g of Hydrogen</u>.

❷ "What mass of Aluminium is produced from 100 tonnes of Aluminium oxide?" A_r : Al = 27, O = 16.

| STEP 1: | Write down the equation. | $2Al_2O_3 \longrightarrow 4Al + 3O_2$ (This would be given) |

| STEP 2: | Calculate M_r of relevant bits. | $2[(2 \times 27) + (3 \times 16)] \longrightarrow 4 \times 27$ Ignore the oxygen. (see above) |

This is ... | THE RATIO OF MASS OF REACTANT ... | 204 $\longrightarrow$ 108 | ... TO MASS OF PRODUCT |

| STEP 3: | Apply this ratio to the question.

If 204 tonnes of Al_2O_3 produces 108 tonnes of Aluminium, ...

... then, 1 tonne of Al_2O_3 produces $\frac{108}{204}$ tonnes of Aluminium, ...

... and, 100 tonnes of Al_2O_3 produces $\frac{108}{204}$ x 100 = <u>52.9 tonnes</u>.

CALCULATING THE MASS OF A REACTANT

"What mass of Calcium carbonate would need to be decomposed to produce 13 tonnes of calcium oxide?" A_r : Ca = 40, C = 12, O = 16.

| STEP 1: | Write down the equation. | $CaCO_3 \longrightarrow CaO + CO_2$ (This would be given) |

| STEP 2: | Calculate M_r of relevant bits. | $40 + 12 + (3 \times 16) \longrightarrow 40 + 16$ Ignore the oxygen. (see above) |

This is ... | THE RATIO OF MASS OF REACTANT ... | 100 $\longrightarrow$ 56 | ... TO MASS OF PRODUCT |

| STEP 3: | Apply this ratio to the question.

If 100 tonnes of $CaCo_3$ produces 56 tonnes of Calcium oxide, ...

... then, $\frac{100}{56}$ tonnes produce 1 tonne of Calcium oxide, ...

... and $\frac{100}{56}$ x 13 tonnes produce 13 tonnes of Calcium oxide.

i.e. <u>23.2 tonnes of Calcium carbonate is needed</u>.

HIGHER TIER

* The mass of the product formed or reactant used up can be calculated for any reaction if we compare the ratio of mass of reactant to mass of product.

CALCULATING THE VOLUME OF GAS PRODUCED

- Firstly the mass of gas is calculated in exactly the same way as on the previous page.
- Then, the mass of the gas must be converted into a volume, using this fact ...

> ... THE RELATIVE FORMULA MASS (M_r) OF A GAS IN GRAMS OCCUPIES A VOLUME OF 24 LITRES ...
> ... AT ORDINARY PRESSURE AND TEMPERATURE.

In other words 2 grams of Hydrogen (H_2), 32 grams of Oxygen (O_2) and 44 grams of Carbon Dioxide (CO_2) all occupy a volume of 24 litres at ordinary pressure and temperature.

EXAMPLE "Find the volume of Ammonia formed when 1.5g of Ammonium Chloride is heated."
A_r: N = 14, H = 1, Cl = 35.

STEP 1: Write down the equation. $NH_4Cl \longrightarrow NH_3 + HCl$

STEP 2: Calculate M_r of relevant bits. $14+(1\times4)+35 \longrightarrow 14+(1\times3)$ Ignore the HCl

This is ... THE RATIO OF MASS OF REACTANT ...   53 $\longrightarrow$ 17   ... TO MASS OF PRODUCT

STEP 3: Apply this ratio to the question: If 53g would produce 17g of ammonia, ...

... then 1g would produce $\frac{17}{53}$ g of ammonia, ...

... and 1.5g would produce $\frac{17}{53} \times 1.5$ = **0.48g of Ammonia.**

STEP 4: Convert this mass to a volume. M_r of a gas in grams occupies 24 litres.

∴ if 17g of ammonia would occupy 24 litres, ...

... then 1g of ammonia would occupy $\frac{24}{17}$ litres, ...

... and 0.48g of ammonia would occupy $\frac{24}{17} \times 0.48$ = **0.67 litres or 670cm³.**

DETERMINING EMPIRICAL FORMULA

The Empirical Formula is the simplest formula which represents the RATIO OF ATOMS IN A COMPOUND.
There's one simple rule ...

> ALWAYS DIVIDE THE DATA YOU ARE GIVEN BY THE A_r OF THE ELEMENT.

EXAMPLE 1 "Find the simplest formula of an oxide of Iron, formed by reacting 2.24g of Iron with 0.96g of Oxygen." (A_r: Fe = 56, O = 16.)

STEP 1: Divide masses by A_r.   For Iron $\frac{2.24}{56}$ = 0.04   For Oxygen $\frac{0.96}{16}$ = 0.06

STEP 2: Simplify this ratio.   0.04 : 0.06   becomes   2 : 3

STEP 3: Write formula.   Simplest formula = Fe_2O_3

EXAMPLE 2 "Find the simplest formula of an oxide of Magnesium which contains 60% Magnesium and 40% Oxygen by weight ." (A_r: Mg = 24, O = 16.) Just treat the percentages as if they were grams ...

STEP 1: Divide masses by A_r.   For Magnesium $\frac{60}{24}$ = 2.5   For Oxygen $\frac{40}{16}$ = 2.5

STEP 2: Simplify this ratio.   2.5 : 2.5   becomes   1 : 1

STEP 3: Write formula.   Simplest formula = MgO

- The relative formula mass (M_r) of a gas in grams occupies a volume of 24 litres at ordinary pressure and temperature.
- The empirical formula is the simplest formula which represents the ratio of atoms in a particular compound.

The Ionic bond.

- This occurs between a metal and non-metal atom.
- And involves a transfer of electrons from one atom to the other.
- to form electrically charged 'atoms called Ions.
- each of which has a 'complete' outer electron cell.

Example Sodium + Chlorine to form Sodium Chloride

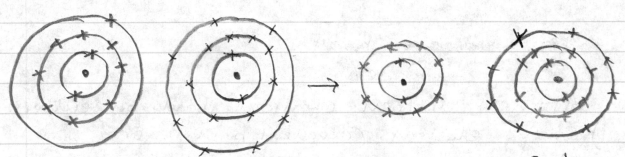

Na Atom
(1 electron in outer shell)
2, 8, 1.

Cl Atom
(7 electrons in outer shell)
2, 8, 7.

Na Ion
$(2,8)^+$

Cl^- Ion
$(2,8,8)^-$

- The Sodium (Na) Atom has 1 electron in its outer shell..
- .. which is TRANSFERRED to the chlorine (Cl) atom.
- Both now have 8 electrons in their outer shell
- The atoms are now IONS
- Na^+ and Cl^-
- and the compound formed is ..
- Sodium Chloride, NaCl.

Chemistry Paper.

Isotopes. - Are atoms of an element that have the same number of protons but different numbers of neutrons.

Helium,   Mass number and
                Proton number.

Number of protons
and neutrons. $^4_2 He$ element Symbol.

Proton number
Number of protons only

~~The~~ ~~combined~~ ~~thinks~~

Bonds.

Atoms can form chemical bonds by either..
1) Sharing electrons (covalent bonds), or...
2) Gaining or losing electrons (ionic bonds)

The covalent bond.
- Occurs between Non-Metal atoms and forms a very strong bond in which electrons are shared.

- Atoms which share electrons often form MOLECULES, in which there are
- STRONG CHEMICAL BONDS BETWEEN THE ATOMS IN EACH MOLECULE, but NOT between SEPARATE MOLECULES.
- This means they usually have low melting and boiling points.
However...
- atoms which share electrons can also form GIANT STRUCTURES e.g diamond
- They have high melting and boiling points.

The Periodic Table.

- The Alkali Metals (Group 1)

- There are 6 metals in this group....
- But the top 3 in the group are the ones we need to deal with..
- especially SODIUM, Na and Potassium, K.

- React with non-metals to form Ionic Compounds

- React with water releasing hydrogen.

- Have lower melting and boiling points as we go down the group.

- The Halogens (Group 7)

- There are 5 ~~metals~~ Non-Metals in this group.

- All have coloured vapours.

- Exist as Molecules made up of pairs of atoms.

- React with metals to form Ionic salts.
- As you move down the group the metals become less reactive
- Can form Compounds with other non-metalic elements
- Can displace less reactive halogens from Aqueous solutions of their salts.
- Have higher melting and boiling points as we go down the groups.

- The Noble gases - Group 0
(Sometimes called
group 8)

There are 6 gases in this group.
- They exist as individual Atoms
(Monatomic)
e.g. He, Ar, Kr etc rather than in
pairs (Diatomic)
like other gaseous elements (Cl_2 H_2 etc)

- Are chemically unreactive.

The Transition Metals

They are the middle section without
numbers for example Fe, Ni, Ag, Hg.

Transition metals have.
- High melting pots.
- Can be often used as catalysts.
- Form colored compounds.

Exo/Endothermic reactions -
- In an exothermic reaction heat is
transferred to the surroundings.
- Combustion is an exothermic reaction
- In an endothermic reaction there
is a transfer of heat from
the surroundings.

Plastics.

- Are a tangled mass of very long molecules in which the Atoms are Joined by strong covalent bonds to form long chains called Polymers.

Atoms

strong covalent bond.

cross links between chains.

A <u>thermosoftening</u> plastic will
- Soften when heated and harden when cooled as the
- Forces between chains are weak.
- These plastics can be moulded.

A <u>thermosetting</u> plastic will
- When heated form covalent bonds between adjacent chains.
- Causing strong cross links which mean.
- that the plastics will not soften when reheated.
- These plastics cannot be remoulded.

- Hydrocarbons.
- Crude oil is a mixture of compounds most of which.
- are molecules made up of carbon and hydrogen atoms only, called HYDROCARBONS. These hydrocarbon molecules vary in size this affects their properties.
- The larger the hydrocarbon.
- The less easily it flows ie the more viscous it is.
- The less easily it ignites i.e. the less flammable it is.
- The less volatile it is. i.e. it doesn't vapourise as easily.
- The higher its boiling point.

Alkenes - Unsaturated hydrocarbons.
- Carbon atoms can also form double covalent bonds with other atoms.
- When the carbon atoms in the 'spine' of the hydrocarbon have
- At least one double covalent bond.
- We say the hydrocarbon is unsaturated and it is known as an Alkene.

Polymers.
- The small alkene molecules above can be described as monomers.
- When lots of monomers join together they form a polymer.
- Because alkenes are unsaturated, they are very good at joining together and
- When they do so without producing another substance we call this
- ADDITION POLYMERISATION.

Displacement reaction - Thermit Reaction.

Iron (III) Oxide + Aluminium → Aluminium Oxide + Iron.

The Aluminium is more reactive than the compound so pushes the Iron out.

Processes of extraction available -
electrolysis - decomposition of substance using electric charge
Reduction - removal of oxygen or other non-metal element from compound.
Blast Furnace - ① Coke + Oxygen → Carbon dioxide.
② Carbon dioxide + coke → carbon monoxide
REDOX REACTION ③ Iron oxide + carbon monoxide → Iron + carbon dioxide
(reduced) (oxidised)

Electrolysis is the breaking down of a compound containing IONS (charged particles) ...

... into its ELEMENTS by using an ELECTRIC CURRENT.

BALANCING HALF-EQUATIONS

During electrolysis ions gain or lose electrons at the electrodes ...

... forming ELECTRICALLY NEUTRAL ATOMS or MOLECULES which are then released. (i.e. they have no charge)

In the example shown, ...

AT THE POSITIVE ELECTRODE Chloride IONS give up an electron and form chlorine MOLECULES ...

$Cl^- - e^- \longrightarrow Cl_2$

AT THE NEGATIVE ELECTRODE Copper IONS pick up TWO electrons and become copper ATOMS ...

$Cu^{2+} + 2e^- \longrightarrow Cu$

The reactions occurring at the electrodes are called **THE HALF EQUATIONS**, but the top one clearly needs balancing since there is only one Cl on the left hand side and two on the right!

$2Cl^- - 2e^- \longrightarrow Cl_2$ (You NEED TO BE ABLE TO BALANCE HALF EQUATIONS!)

ELECTROLYSIS OF COPPER CHLORIDE SOLUTION

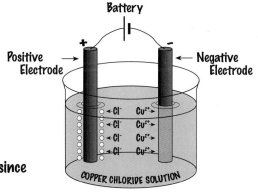

HIGHER TIER

CALCULATION OF MASS/VOLUME OF THE PRODUCTS OF ELECTROLYSIS

Here's a typical question ... "If 1.0g of Copper is deposited at the negative electrode during the electrolysis of Copper chloride, calculate the volume of chlorine released."

STEP 1: Write down the half equations occurring at the electrodes ...

CATHODE: $Cu^{2+} + 2e^- \longrightarrow Cu_{(s)}$

ANODE: $2 Cl^- - 2e^- \longrightarrow Cl_{2(g)}$ (CHLORINE EXISTS AS MOLECULES!)

STEP 2: So, same amount of charge (2e-) liberates 1 atom of Copper, and 1 molecule of chlorine.

But since the A_r of Cu is 63, and the A_r of Cl is 35, this means that ...

... 63g of Copper, and 70g (2 x 35!) of Chlorine (the M_r) are liberated by the same amount of charge.

THESE TWO FIGURES (63g and 70g) REPRESENT THE <u>RELATIVE MASSES</u> LIBERATED BY THE SAME CHARGE so, to get the ACTUAL MASS we use the following formula ...

$$\frac{\text{ACTUAL MASS OF CHLORINE LIBERATED}}{\text{ACTUAL MASS OF COPPER LIBERATED}} = \frac{\text{RELATIVE MASS OF CHLORINE LIBERATED}}{\text{RELATIVE MASS OF COPPER LIBERATED}}$$

Inserting figures, ... $\frac{x}{1.0} = \frac{70}{63}$; $x = \frac{70}{63} \times 1.0$; $x = 1.11g$ of Chlorine are liberated.

STEP 3: Convert this to a volume, by using this very important fact ... "At room temperature and pressure, the Relative Formula Mass of a gas (M_r), in grams occupies a volume of 24 litres."

Therefore, $\text{VOLUME OF GAS} = \frac{24 \times \text{MASS OF GAS (g)}}{\text{RELATIVE FORMULA MASS } (M_r) \text{ OF GAS (g)}}$

In this case, $\text{VOLUME OF CHLORINE} = \frac{24 \times 1.11}{70}$, VOL. OF CHLORINE = 0.381 litre or 381 cm³

* IMPORTANT POINT!

In cases where the same charge doesn't liberate the same amounts e.g. ...

... $2H^+(aq) + 2e^- = H_2(g)$ and $O^{2-}(aq) - 2e^- = O(g)$, use the exact relative mass

i.e. in this case, H_2 would be 2, and O would be 16 (<u>not</u> 32!)

HIGHER TIER

• For electrolysis calculations firstly write down balanced half-equations and then use the formula:

$$\frac{\text{Actual Mass Of Substance A Liberated}}{\text{Actual Mass Of Substance B Liberated}} = \frac{\text{Relative Mass Of Substance A Liberated}}{\text{Relative Mass Of Substance B Liberated}}$$

- Chemical reactions only occur when REACTING PARTICLES COLLIDE WITH EACH OTHER ...
- ... with sufficient energy to react.
- The minimum amount of energy required to cause this reaction is called the ACTIVATION ENERGY.
- There are 4 important factors which affect RATE OF REACTION, ...

1. TEMPERATURE OF THE REACTANTS
When temperature increases, the particles MOVE FASTER ...

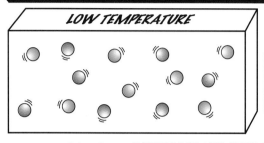
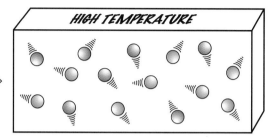

- ... resulting in an INCREASED NUMBER OF COLLISIONS, and an INCREASED RATE OF REACTIONS.
- Also, the particles collide more energetically and therefore are more likely to react.

2. CONCENTRATION OF THE REACTANTS
Increased concentration means an increased number of particles ...

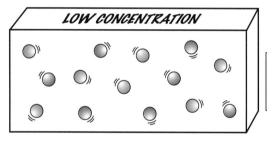
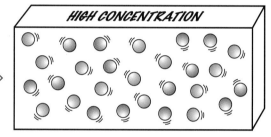

- ... resulting in an INCREASED NUMBER OF COLLISIONS, and an INCREASED RATE OF REACTION.
- Increasing the PRESSURE of reacting GASES also increases the concentration of particles and the rate of reaction.

3. SURFACE AREA OF SOLID REACTANTS
Smaller pieces means a greater area for contact ...

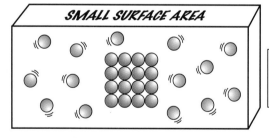
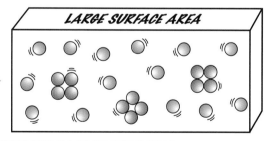

- ... resulting in an INCREASED NUMBER OF COLLISIONS, and an INCREASED RATE OF REACTION.
- Reactions can only take place at the exposed, outer surface of the solid.

4. USE OF A CATALYST

A catalyst is a substance which ...
- ... INCREASES THE RATE OF A CHEMICAL REACTION, WITHOUT BEING USED UP IN THE PROCESS.
- CATALYSTS are SPECIFIC, i.e. DIFFERENT REACTIONS NEED DIFFERENT CATALYSTS.

    Examples   1. The cracking of hydrocarbons using BROKEN POTTERY!
                2. The manufacture of ammonia (Haber Process) using IRON.

Increasing the rates of chemical reactions is important in industry because it helps to reduce costs.

- Temperature of the reactants, concentration of the reactants, surface area of solid reactants and use of a catalyst are four factors which affect rate of reaction.

ANALYSING RATE OF REACTION

The rate of a chemical reaction can be analysed by measuring ...

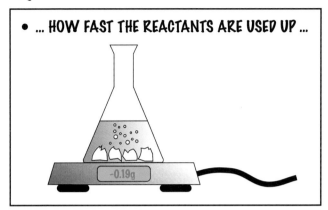

• ... HOW FAST THE PRODUCTS ARE FORMED ...   or,   • ... HOW FAST THE REACTANTS ARE USED UP ...

By measuring either of the above against time, a graph can be produced ...
• The slope (gradient) of the graph is GREATER AT THE BEGINNING ...
• ... when there are MORE REACTANTS to collide with each other.
• It then steadily DECREASES as the reactants are used up.
In the graph alongside, ...
... REACTION 'A' WAS COMPLETED FASTER THAN REACTION 'B' ...
... due to one of the following factors ...

| GREATER TEMPERATURE IN A | , | GREATER CONCENTRATION OF REACTANTS IN A | , |

| GREATER SURFACE AREA OF REACTANTS IN A | , | USE OF A CATALYST IN A. |

ENZYME ACTIVITY AND TEMPERATURE

• ENZYMES are BIOLOGICAL CATALYSTS ... contained within LIVING CELLS.
• They are PROTEIN MOLECULES ... and extremely important ...
• ... e.g. every reaction in our body is CATALYSED by ENZYMES ...
The graph alongside shows the effect of temperature ...
... on enzyme activity.
As the temperature rises, increased collisions between reactants and enzymes increase the enzyme activity up to the optimum temperature. After this, the increase in temperature continues to cause increased collisions but the enzyme molecules are permanently damaged by the heat resulting in decreased enzyme activity.

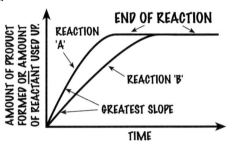

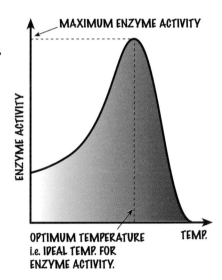

USE OF ENZYMES IN THE FOOD INDUSTRY

1. FERMENTATION
• ANAEROBIC RESPIRATION (without oxygen) controlled by enzymes in YEAST CELLS provides ETHANOL (alcohol) and CARBON DIOXIDE.   GLUCOSE ⟶ ETHANOL + CARBON DIOXIDE
• The ETHANOL is used as the basis for the BREWING and WINE MAKING INDUSTRIES.
• The CARBON DIOXIDE is used in BAKING to make the bread rise.   CARBON DIOXIDE TURNS LIMEWATER MILKY!!
2. YOGHURT PRODUCTION
• Enzymes in bacteria produce YOGURT from MILK by converting the sugar (LACTOSE) ...
• ... to LACTIC ACID (so giving it a slightly sour taste)

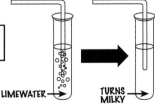

• The rate of reaction can be analysed by measuring how fast products are formed or reactants used up.
• Enzymes are biological catalysts whose activity depends on temperature.

BURNING FUELS – EXOTHERMIC REACTIONS

When fuels are burned, energy is released as heat. This is COMBUSTION.

EXAMPLES :-

Methane (natural gas)   +   Oxygen   ⟶   Carbon dioxide + water   **+ HEAT ENERGY**

Ethanol (methylated spirits)   +   Oxygen   ⟶   Carbon dioxide + water   **+ HEAT ENERGY**

Carbon (coal)   +   Oxygen   ⟶   Carbon dioxide   **+ HEAT ENERGY**

Butane (Camping gas)   +   Oxygen   ⟶   Carbon dioxide + water   **+ HEAT ENERGY**

Octane (in petrol)   +   Oxygen   ⟶   Carbon dioxide + water   **+ HEAT ENERGY**

- These are all examples of chemical reactions which
  TRANSFER HEAT TO THE SURROUNDINGS ...
- ... i.e. they are **EXOTHERMIC REACTIONS.**
- It is not only reactions between fuels and oxygen which are exothermic! For example neutralising alkalis with acids gives out heat too!

TAKING IN HEAT – ENDOTHERMIC REACTIONS

EXAMPLE Dissolving ammonium nitrate in water.

Ammonium nitrate   +   water ⟶ ammonium nitrate solution   -   HEAT ENERGY
(Minus)

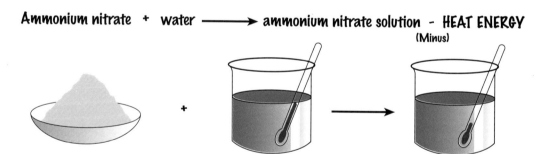

The temperature here has fallen by 7°C!

- The heat energy is taken from the water by the ammonium nitrate ...
  ... so the temperature of the water falls.
- The water then takes heat energy from the surroundings as it returns to room temperature.
- In this reaction, there is a TRANSFER OF HEAT FROM THE SURROUNDINGS ...
- ... i.e. it is an **ENDOTHERMIC REACTION.**

> **YOU DON'T NEED TO KNOW THE DETAILS OF THESE REACTIONS BUT YOU MUST UNDERSTAND THE PRINCIPLES OF EXOTHERMIC AND ENDOTHERMIC REACTIONS.**

- In an exothermic reaction heat is transferred to the surroundings.
- Combustion is an exothermic reaction.
- In an endothermic reaction there is a transfer of heat from the surroundings.

EXOTHERMIC AND ENDOTHERMIC REACTIONS

Two very important points ...

1. ENERGY MUST BE <u>SUPPLIED</u> TO BREAK CHEMICAL BONDS ...

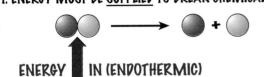

ENERGY IN (ENDOTHERMIC)

2. ENERGY IS <u>RELEASED</u> WHEN CHEMICAL BONDS ARE FORMED.

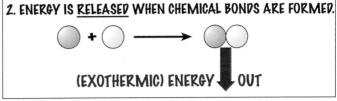

(EXOTHERMIC) ENERGY OUT

So, in reactions where bonds are broken and then new bonds are formed, two things may occur ...

| THE ENERGY NEEDED TO BREAK EXISTING BONDS ... | can be GREATER than ... | ... THE ENERGY RELEASED FROM FORMING NEW BONDS ... | and so ... | ... the REACTION is ENDOTHERMIC. |

or

| THE ENERGY NEEDED TO BREAK EXISTING BONDS ... | can be LESS than ... | ... THE ENERGY RELEASED FROM FORMING NEW BONDS ... | and so ... | ... the REACTION is EXOTHERMIC. |

ENERGY LEVEL DIAGRAMS – e.g. the reaction of methane with oxygen

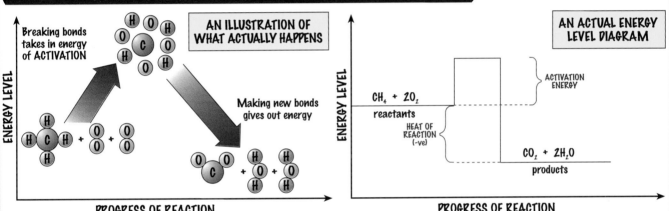

The energy level diagram first of all rises as ACTIVATION ENERGY is put in to start the reaction (i.e. a match is struck!) Then the energy level falls as heat energy is given out in this exothermic reaction. The HEAT of REACTION is the difference between the energy of the products and the energy of the reactants, and is always NEGATIVE FOR EXOTHERMIC REACTIONS and POSITIVE FOR ENDOTHERMIC REACTIONS.

TWO MORE EXAMPLES OF ENERGY LEVEL DIAGRAMS:

USING A CATALYST REDUCES THE AMOUNT OF ACTIVATION ENERGY WHICH IS NEEDED TO START THE REACTION.

with a catalyst

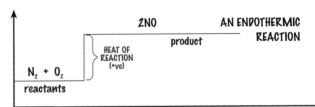

2NO product — AN ENDOTHERMIC REACTION

HEAT OF REACTION (+ve)

$N_2 + O_2$ reactants

CALCULATING NETT ENERGY TRANSFERS USING GIVEN BOND ENERGIES

Scientists have calculated the different amounts of energy involved in various chemical bonds. To work out whether a reaction is ENDO, or EXOTHERMIC all we have to do is substitute these figures.

TYPICAL QUESTION: "Use the data in the table to calculate the NETT ENERGY. TRANSFERRED when methane reacts with oxygen. $CH_4 + 2O_2 \rightarrow CO_2 + 2H_2O$

BOND ENERGIES	
C – H	435
O = O	497 (units may vary)
C = O	803
H – O	464

BOND BREAKING

CH_4 + $2O_2$

(4 x 435) + (2 x 497)

2734 KJ

BOND MAKING

CO_2 + $2H_2O$

(2 x 803) + (4 x 464)

3462 KJ = -728 KJ i.e. it is EXOTHERMIC

HIGHER TIER

- In an exothermic reaction energy is released when chemical bonds are formed.
- In an endothermic reaction energy must be supplied to break chemical bonds.
- Activation energy is the energy needed to start a reaction.
- Heat of reaction is the difference between the energy of the products and the energy of the reactants.

You should know the formulae of SIMPLE IONIC COMPOUNDS, and SIMPLE COVALENT COMPOUNDS which are referred to in the tier for which you are entered (i.e. Higher and Foundation).

FORMULAE OF COMMON IONS

In the examination you will be given the following ionic formulae to help you, but it's better to familiarise yourself with them now.

HYDROGEN H^+	AMMONIUM NH_4^+	ZINC Zn^{2+}	CHLORIDE Cl^-	NITRATE NO_3^-
SODIUM Na^+	BARIUM Ba^{2+}	LEAD Pb^{2+}	BROMIDE Br^-	OXIDE O^{2-}
SILVER Ag^+	CALCIUM Ca^{2+}	IRON (II) Fe^{2+}	FLUORIDE F^-	SULPHIDE S^{2-}
POTASSIUM K^+	COPPER (II) Cu^{2+}	IRON (III) Fe^{3+}	IODIDE I^-	SULPHATE SO_4^{2-}
LITHIUM Li^+	MAGNESIUM Mg^{2+}	ALUMINIUM Al^{3+}	HYDROXIDE OH^-	CARBONATE CO_3^{2-}

A good exercise is to try "pairing up" positive and negative ions in a BALANCED FORMULA.
All you really have to do is balance the positive and negative 'signs'.
Try to complete this table; some have already been done for you.

	CHLORIDE Cl^-	HYDROXIDE OH^-	OXIDE O^{2-}	SULPHIDE S^{2-}	CARBONATE CO_3^{2-}	NITRATE NO_3^-
POTASSIUM K^+		KOH				
CALCIUM Ca^{2+}						$Ca(NO_3)_2$
IRON (III) Fe^{3+}			Fe_2O_3			

HAZARD SYMBOLS

Candidates should be able to recognise, and explain the significance of the following symbols:

Oxidising
These substances provide oxygen which allows other materials to burn more fiercely.

Example: ------------------------------

Harmful
These substances are similar to toxic substances but less dangerous.

Example: ------------------------------

Highly flammable
These substances easily catch fire.

Example: ------------------------------

Corrosive
These substances attack and destroy living tissues, including eyes and skin.

Example: ------------------------------

Toxic
These can cause death and may have an effect when swallowed, breathed in or absorbed through the skin.

Example: ------------------------------

Irritant
These substances are not corrosive but can cause reddening or blistering of the skin.

Example: ------------------------------

• You should be able to state ONE EXAMPLE of each type of hazardous substance.

• The six hazard symbols are:
Oxidising, Highly Flammable, Toxic, Harmful, Corrosive and Irritant.

Please refer to the Periodic Table for A_r of substances involved.

1. In terms of elements present, and numbers of atoms involved, what do the following formulae represent?
    $$Ca(OH)_2, \qquad KNO_3, \qquad Na_2CO_3$$

2. Explain what the state symbols are and give an example of an equation with them in.

3. Write down the formulae for the following simple ionic compounds ...
    Sodium Chloride, Magnesium Oxide, Sulphuric Acid, Sodium Hydroxide and Calcium Carbonate.

4. Write balanced symbol equations for the following reactions:
    Potassium   +   Water $\longrightarrow$ Potassium Hydroxide   +   Hydrogen
    Sodium Hydroxide   +   Sulphuric Acid $\longrightarrow$ Potassium Sulphate   +   Water
    Hydrogen   +   Chlorine $\longrightarrow$ Hydrogen Chloride

5. Calculate the Relative Formula Mass of the following compounds:
Water, H_2O	Ammonia, NH_3
Carbon Dioxide, CO_2	Sodium Chloride, $NaCl$
Methane, CH_4	Sodium Carbonate, Na_2CO_3
Nitrogen, N_2	Ammonium Chloride, NH_4Cl

6. What is the essential difference between Relative Atomic Mass and Relative Formula Mass?

7. Calculate the Relative Formula Masses of all the compounds in the following symbol equation ...
    $$NaOH \quad + \quad HCl \longrightarrow NaCl \quad + \quad H_2O$$

8. Calculate the percentage mass of Oxygen in Water, H_2O.

9. Calculate the percentage mass of Oxygen in Carbon Dioxide, CO_2.

10. Calculate the percentage mass of Carbon in Methane, CH_4.

11. Calculate the percentage mass of Nitrogen in Ammonia, NH_3.

12. Calculate the percentage mass of Chlorine in Sodium Chloride, $NaCl$.

13. Calculate the percentage mass of Oxygen in Sodium Carbonate, Na_2CO_3.

14. Calculate the percentage mass of Hydrogen in Ammonium Chloride, NH_4Cl.

15. What mass of Aluminium is produced by the electrolysis of **38.5** tonnes of Aluminium Oxide?
    $$2Al_2O_{3(s)} \longrightarrow 4Al_{(s)} \quad + \quad 3O_{2(g)}$$

16. What mass of Calcium Oxide is produced by the thermal decomposition of **27** tonnes of Calcium Carbonate?
    $$CaCO_{3(s)} \longrightarrow CaO_{(s)} \quad + \quad CO_{2(g)}$$

17. What mass of Hydrogen Chloride gas is produced by the thermal decomposition of 6.0g of Ammonium Chloride?
    $$NH_4Cl_{(s)} \longrightarrow NH_{3(g)} \quad + \quad HCl_{(g)}$$

18. What mass of Copper is produced from the electrolysis of 87g of Copper Chloride?
    $$CuCl_{2(aq)} \longrightarrow Cu_{(s)} \quad + \quad Cl_{2(g)}$$

19. What mass of Calcium Carbonate would need to be decomposed to produce 27 kilograms of Calcium Oxide?
$$CaCO_3 \longrightarrow CaO + CO_2$$

20. Find the volume of Ammonia formed when 7.5g of Ammonium Chloride is heated.
$$NH_4Cl_{(s)} \longrightarrow NH_{3(g)} + HCl_{(g)}$$

21. Find the simplest formula of a chloride of Sodium formed by reacting 4.6g of Sodium with 7.0g of Chloride (A_r: Na = 23, Cl = 35).

22. Find the simplest formula of an oxide of Carbon formed by reacting 1.2g of Carbon with 3.2g of Oxygen (A_r: C = 12, O = 16).

23. Balance the following half equation: $$O^{2-} - 2e^- \longrightarrow O_2$$

24. If 2.3g of Copper is deposited at the negative electrode during electrolysis of Copper Chloride, calculate the mass and volume of Chlorine released.

25. Write down the FOUR factors which affect rate of chemical reaction. For any TWO of these explain how reaction rate is affected.

26. a) Describe how you could monitor the rate of a chemical reaction against time.
    b) Draw a graph of enzyme activity against temperature.

27. a) What are exothermic and endothermic reactions
    b) Write TWO word equations for exothermic reactions.

28. a) Comment in as much detail as possible on the energy level diagram (i).

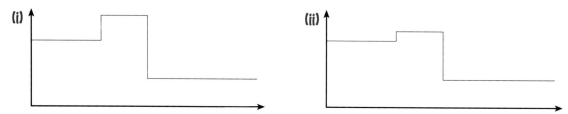

    b) Diagram (ii) is for the same reaction. Explain what could have caused the change.

29. Calculate the nett energy transfer when Carbon reacts with Oxygen to form Carbon Dioxide (Bond energies: O = O 497, C = O 803).

30. Draw a table showing how positive ions of Lithium, Copper and Magnesium react with negative Chloride and Carbonate ions.

Earth Science

- When a substance burns it reacts with OXYGEN ...
- ... to produce compounds called OXIDES.
- When a FOSSIL FUEL burns ...
- ... WASTE PRODUCTS are formed which are released into the ATMOSPHERE.

- Because these fuels contain CARBON, HYDROGEN and SULPHUR ...
- ... the waste products include CARBON DIOXIDE, WATER VAPOUR (an oxide of hydrogen) ...
- ... and SULPHUR DIOXIDE.

CARBON DIOXIDE   WATER VAPOUR

Methane →   ← Oxygen

EXAMPLE

NATURAL GAS is made up mainly of METHANE ...

> METHANE   +   OXYGEN ⟶ CARBON DIOXIDE   +   WATER VAPOUR   +   HEAT

... and if SULPHUR is present in the fuel ...

> SULPHUR   +   OXYGEN ⟶ SULPHUR DIOXIDE

GLOBAL WARMING – Effects of increasing Carbon Dioxide

- CARBON DIOXIDE is one of the "GREENHOUSE GASES."
- The INCREASED BURNING OF FUELS ...
- ... is INCREASING the LEVELS of CARBON DIOXIDE ...
- ... in the ATMOSPHERE which is resulting in GLOBAL WARMING.

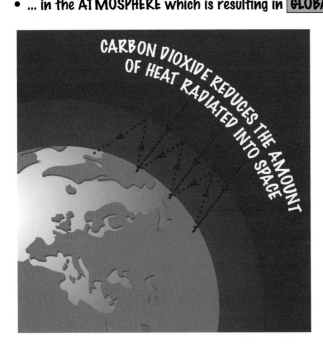

CARBON DIOXIDE REDUCES THE AMOUNT OF HEAT RADIATED INTO SPACE

- Light from the Sun reaches the Earth ...
- ... and passes through the atmosphere.
- This WARMS up the planet which ...
- ... then radiates this heat energy back into SPACE.

- CARBON DIOXIDE helps to trap some of this energy ...
- ... which helps to keep the planet WARM.
- Too much carbon dioxide however leads to ...
- ... too much heat being retained.
- This is GLOBAL WARMING.

- Methane + Oxygen ⟶ Carbon dioxide + Water Vapour + Heat
- Sulphur + Oxygen ⟶ Sulphur dioxide
- Increased burning of fuels is increasing the level of carbon dioxide in the atmosphere resulting in global warming.

ACID RAIN – Effects of Sulphur Dioxide and Nitrogen Oxides

- $\boxed{\text{SULPHUR DIOXIDE}}$ and $\boxed{\text{NITROGEN OXIDES}}$ are produced ...
- ... when FUELS are burned in FURNACES and ENGINES (mainly cars).
- These gases then react with $\boxed{\text{WATER VAPOUR}}$ in the ATMOSPHERE ...
- ... to produce ACIDS.
- These fall as ACID RAIN.

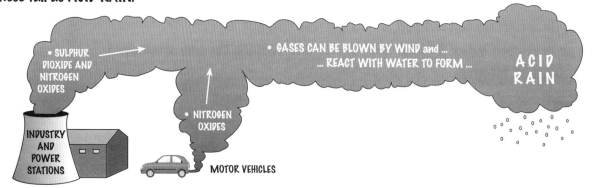

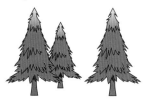

The GASES themselves can harm PLANTS and ANIMALS directly ...

... and cause EROSION damage to ...
... STONE and METALWORK of BUILDINGS ...

... while ACID RAIN causes LAKES and RIVERS ...
... to become so ACIDIC that ...
... PLANTS and ANIMALS cannot survive!! ...

... it also causes EROSION damage to ...
... STONE and METALWORK of BUILDINGS.

COMPOSITION OF THE ATMOSPHERE

Our atmosphere has been more or less the same for 200 million years!!!

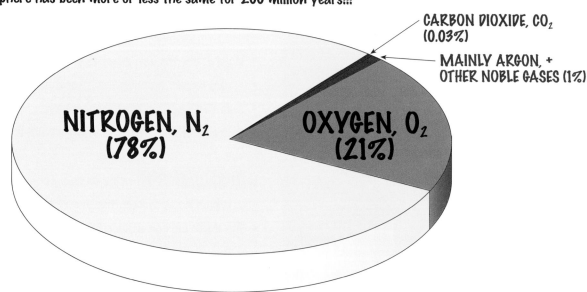

CARBON DIOXIDE, CO_2 (0.03%)

MAINLY ARGON, + OTHER NOBLE GASES (1%)

NITROGEN, N_2 (78%)

OXYGEN, O_2 (21%)

- $\boxed{\text{WATER VAPOUR}}$ may also be present in varying quantities (0 - 3%).

- Sulphur dioxide and nitrogen oxides react with water vapour in the atmosphere to produce Acid Rain.
- The atmosphere is made from Nitrogen, Oxygen, Carbon dioxide, Argon (and other Noble gases) and Water vapour.

HIGHER TIER

Our atmosphere has changed dramatically (thank heavens!) since the formation of the Earth 4.6 BILLION years ago. This table gives you the timescale and factors involved in forming our atmosphere.

COMPOSITION OF THE ATMOSPHERE		FORMATION OF THE EARTH	THE FACTORS WHICH AFFECTED OUR ATMOSPHERE

Mainly CARBON DIOXIDE plus WATER VAPOUR and a bit of METHANE and AMMONIA.

Little or no OXYGEN.

4 — AGO

- Volcanoes release ...
- ... mainly CARBON DIOXIDE ...
- ... and small amounts of METHANE and AMMONIA ...
- ... and also WATER VAPOUR ...
- ... which condenses to form the oceans.

← FIRST GREEN PLANTS EVOLVE

3 — YEARS

- CARBON DIOXIDE reduced as ...
- ... plants take in CARBON DIOXIDE and give out OXYGEN.
- Micro-organisms which could not tolerate OXYGEN ...
- ... are killed off.
- CARBON from the CARBON DIOXIDE in the air ...
- ... becomes locked up in sedimentary rocks as carbonates ...
- ... and fossil fuels.
- METHANE and AMMONIA in the atmosphere ...
- ... react with the OXYGEN causing the ...
- ... release of NITROGEN into the air (from the ammonia) ...
- ... Nitrogen is also produced ...
- ... by the action of DENITRIFYING BACTERIA ...
- ... on nitrates from decaying plant material.

CARBON DIOXIDE, METHANE and AMMONIA decreasing ...

OXYGEN and NITROGEN increasing.

2 — OF

1 — BILLIONS

... and decreasing.

OXYGEN and NITROGEN nearly up to present levels 20% OXYGEN, 78% NITROGEN.

- Free OXYGEN increases, and OZONE LAYER forms.
- OZONE filters out harmful U-V light from the Sun ...
- ... allowing the evolution ...
- ... of new land living organisms.

NOW

An important point here! These are BILLIONS of years i.e. a thousand million!!

MODERN DAY CHANGES TO THE LEVEL OF CARBON DIOXIDE IN THE ATMOSPHERE

1.
- Geological activity moves CARBONATE ROCKS ...
- ... deep into the Earth.
- During volcanic activity ...
- ... they may release CARBON DIOXIDE ...
- ... back into the atmosphere.

2.
- Level of CARBON DIOXIDE ...
- ... in the atmosphere ...
- ... is INCREASING through ...
- ... the burning of the CARBON ...
- ... locked up in FOSSIL FUELS.

Also ...
3.
- Increased CARBON DIOXIDE in the atmosphere increases the reaction between ...
- ... CARBON DIOXIDE and SEA WATER which produces ...
- ... SOLUBLE CARBONATES (mainly CALCIUM) which are deposited as SEDIMENT, ...
- ... and SOLUBLE HYDROCARBONATES (mainly CALCIUM and MAGNESIUM).
- But even so the level of CARBON DIOXIDE continues to rise!!

HIGHER TIER

- The composition of the atmosphere 4.6 billion years ago was mainly carbon dioxide plus water vapour and small amounts of methane and ammonia.
- Geological activity and burning increase the level of carbon dioxide in the atmosphere.

The basic facts about the FORMATION, CHARACTERISTICS, and SPECIFIC FEATURES need to be learnt. We've cut out all the waffle so this is all you need to know.

	HOW THEY'RE FORMED	EXAMPLES	SPECIFIC FEATURES OF THESE EXAMPLES	WHAT THEY LOOK LIKE
SEDIMENTARY	• Made from layers of SEDIMENT (small particles) ... • ... whose WEIGHT squeezes out WATER ... • ... causing particles to become "CEMENTED" together ... • ... by SALTS, CRYSTALLISING OUT. • YOUNGER ROCKS therefore are usually ON TOP.	SANDSTONE	Formed by particles of SAND, washed down by river, eventually falling to RIVER BED or SEA BED.	• Very GRAINY and CRUMBLY • SAND-GRAINS OBVIOUS • Sometimes contains FOSSILS ... • ... which can be used to DATE rocks.
		LIMESTONE	Formed by DEAD REMAINS of SHELLED CREATURES and some INSOLUBLE CALCIUM SALTS. e.g. Calcium Carbonate	• GRAINY + CRUMBLY but less than above • Often contain FOSSILS ... • ... which can be used to DATE rocks.
IGNEOUS	• Formed from MOLTEN ROCK ... • ... called MAGMA ... • ... which wells up from the MANTLE ... • ... and COOLS DOWN, either ... • ... ABOVE or WITHIN the earth's crust.	BASALT	Expelled from VOLCANOES. Formed EXTRUSIVELY by cooling, ABOVE the earth's crust.	• Very SMALL CRYSTALS due to FAST COOLING. • Very HARD rocks.
		GRANITE	Magma forced into the earth's crust. Formed INTRUSIVELY by cooling WITHIN the earth's crust.	• LARGE CRYSTALS due to SLOW COOLING • Very HARD rocks.
METAMORPHIC	• Formed by extreme TEMP. and PRESSURE ... • ... caused by MOUNTAIN BUILDING processes ... • ... which force SEDIMENTARY rocks deep underground ... • ... close to MAGMA ... • ... where they become COMPRESSED and HEATED ... • ... changing their TEXTURE and STRUCTURE. • Can be formed from any rock type.	SLATE	Formed when MUDSTONE experiences EXTREME TEMPERATURE and PRESSURE.	• Tiny CRYSTALS form on COOLING • Usually HARD rocks. • Can form BANDS
		MARBLE	Formed when LIMESTONE experiences EXTREME TEMPERATURE and PRESSURE.	• Small CRYSTALS form on COOLING • Usually HARD rocks. • Crystals tend to form BANDS. • BANDING indicates metamorphic rock, eg. Marble, Schist.

• There are three types of rock: Sedimentary, Igneous and Metamorphic.
• Sedimentary rocks are grainy and crumbly and may contain fossils. • Igneous rocks are crystalline and very hard.
• Metamorphic rocks are crystalline and banded.

The ROCK CYCLE is an ongoing CYCLE OF EVENTS where ROCKS at the EARTH'S SURFACE are continually being BROKEN UP, REFORMED and CHANGED.

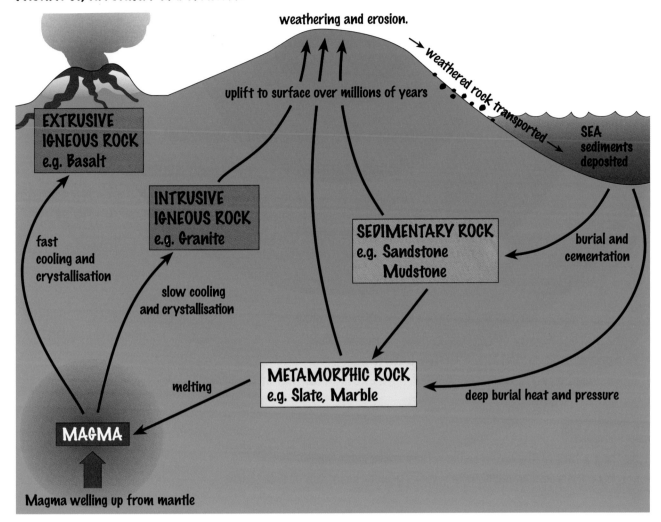

ON THE GROUND SURFACE

Remember the 4 stages involved in formation of SEDIMENTARY ROCKS.
- WEATHERING and EROSION.
- TRANSPORTATION of sediment.
- DEPOSITION of sediment.
- BURIAL of sediment.

BELOW THE GROUND SURFACE

1. Molten MAGMA is crystallised to form
   - INTRUSIVE IGNEOUS ROCKS ...
     ... within the crust.
   - EXTRUSIVE IGNEOUS ROCKS ...
     ... above the crust.

2. SEDIMENTARY ROCKS get close to the MAGMA and form METAMORPHIC ROCKS.

3. All types of rock can return to the MAGMA by being driven underground very deeply.

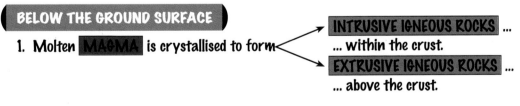

- The four stages involved in the formation of sedimentary rocks are: Weathering and Erosion, Transportation, Deposition and Burial. • Molten magma crystallises to form igneous rocks.
- Metamorphic rocks are formed when sedimentary rocks get close to the magma.

Although there doesn't seem to be much going on, the Earth and its crust are very dynamic.
It's just that things take such a <u>long</u> time.

STRUCTURE OF THE EARTH

The Earth is nearly spherical and has a layered structure as follows where ...

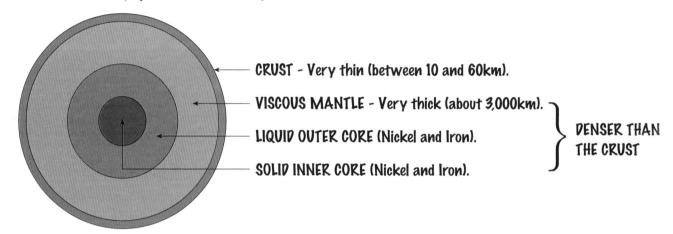

CRUST - Very thin (between 10 and 60km).

VISCOUS MANTLE - Very thick (about 3,000km).

LIQUID OUTER CORE (Nickel and Iron).

SOLID INNER CORE (Nickel and Iron).

} DENSER THAN THE CRUST

- ... the average density of the Earth is <u>MUCH GREATER</u> than ...
- ... the average density of the rocks which form the CRUST.
- This proves that the INTERIOR OF THE EARTH ...
- ... is made of a DIFFERENT and DENSER MATERIAL than that of the crust.

THE CRUST

- At the surface of the Earth sedimentary rocks exist mainly in LAYERS, ...
- ... where the younger sedimentary rocks <u>usually</u> lie on top of older rocks.

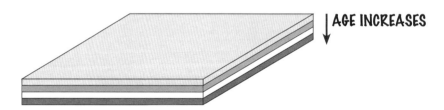

↓ AGE INCREASES

- However, sedimentary rock layers are often found ...

... TILTED ...   ... FOLDED ...   ... FRACTURED ...   ... TURNED UPSIDE DOWN.

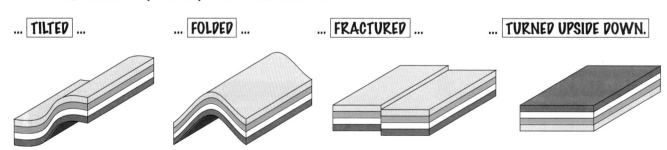

- All this shows ...
- ... that the EARTH'S CRUST HAS BEEN SUBJECTED TO VERY LARGE FORCES ...
- ... to cause this movement of the sedimentary rock layers ...
- ... and is very UNSTABLE!

- The Earth has a layered structure made up of the Crust, Viscous Mantle, Liquid Outer Core and Solid Inner Core.
- The crust is a dynamic structure that can be changed in many ways.

MOVEMENT OF THE CRUST

- The Earth's CRUST is 'cracked' into several large pieces ...
- ... called TECTONIC PLATES ...
- ... which move slowly at speeds of a few cm per year ...
- ... driven by CONVECTION CURRENTS ...
- ... in the MANTLE which are caused ...
- ... by HEAT released from RADIOACTIVE DECAY.

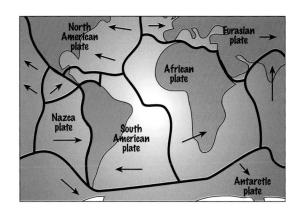

OCEAN FLOOR SPREADING AWAY FROM THIS POINT

CRUST   CRUST

convection currents in the mantle   convection currents in the mantle

HOT MOLTEN ROCK COMING UP TO THE SURFACE AND SPREADING SIDEWAYS SLOWLY!

In other words,
- New crust is formed where the rising convection current reaches the crust ...
- ... and old crust disappears where the convection current starts to fall ...
- ... causing the land masses on these plates to move slowly across the globe!

Also,
- Where two land masses collide, mountain ranges are formed e.g. the Himalayas.
- These take millions of years to form and ...
- ... they replace older mountain ranges ...
- ... which have become worn down by weathering and erosion.

EVIDENCE FOR TECTONIC PLATES

Evidence for the TECTONIC PLATES theory has been gained by comparing the EAST COAST of SOUTH AMERICA and the WEST COAST of AFRICA. Although separated by thousands of kilometres of ocean, they have ...

1. CLOSELY MATCHING SHAPES

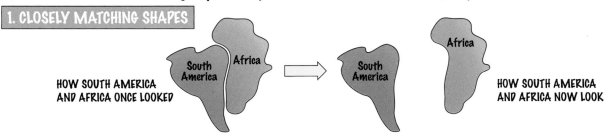

HOW SOUTH AMERICA AND AFRICA ONCE LOOKED

HOW SOUTH AMERICA AND AFRICA NOW LOOK

2. SIMILAR PATTERNS OF ROCKS AND FOSSILS

- ROCKS of the SAME TYPE and AGE have been found ...
- ... which contain FOSSILS of the SAME PLANTS and ANIMALS e.g. the MESOSAURUS.

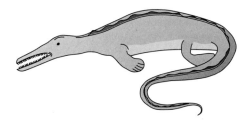

Although ...
People used to believe that the features of the Earth's surface were caused by SHRINKAGE when the Earth cooled!! We now reject this in favour of TECTONIC THEORY which explains MOUNTAIN BUILDING and the movement of the CONTINENTS from how they were (as GONDWANALAND) to what they look like today.

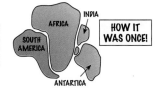

HOW IT WAS ONCE!

> - The Earth's crust is cracked into several large pieces called Tectonic Plates. • Convection currents in the mantle cause these plates to move apart or collide. • Evidence for tectonic plates has been gained by comparing the shape and pattern of rocks and fossils of the East Coast of South America and the West Coast of Africa.

The 'plates' on the previous page can basically only do THREE things.

1. SLIDE PAST EACH OTHER

- When plates SLIDE, HUGE STRESSES AND STRAINS build up in the crust ...
- ... which eventually have to be RELEASED in order that MOVEMENT can occur.
- This 'release' of energy results in an EARTHQUAKE.
- A classic example of this is the West Coast of North America (esp. California).

2. MOVE AWAY FROM EACH OTHER – Constructive plate margins

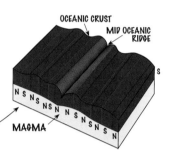

- New rock is formed on the ocean floor at MID OCEANIC RIDGES ...
- ... by MAGMA, in rising CONVECTION CURRENTS starting to cool ...
- ... and spread outwards forming new BASALTIC OCEAN CRUST ...
- ... at a rate of about 2cm PER YEAR.
- As the magma cools, IRON-RICH minerals ORIENTATE themselves ...
- ... in the DIRECTION OF THE EARTH'S MAGNETIC FIELD ...
- ... forming MAGNETIC REVERSAL PATTERNS ...
- ... parallel to the MID OCEANIC RIDGE.
- The magnetic field of the earth has changed NINE times in the past 3.6 million years, and ...
- ... this is 'mirrored' in these REVERSAL PATTERNS.

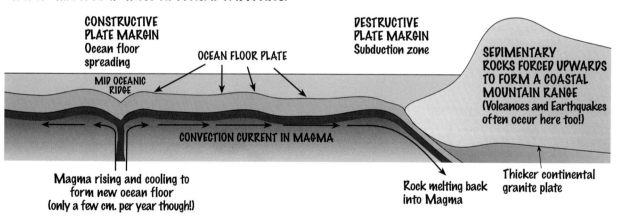

CONSTRUCTIVE PLATE MARGIN
Ocean floor spreading

OCEAN FLOOR PLATE

MID OCEANIC RIDGE

DESTRUCTIVE PLATE MARGIN
Subduction zone

SEDIMENTARY ROCKS FORCED UPWARDS TO FORM A COASTAL MOUNTAIN RANGE
(Volcanoes and Earthquakes often occur here too!)

CONVECTION CURRENT IN MAGMA

Magma rising and cooling to form new ocean floor
(only a few cm. per year though!)

Rock melting back into Magma

Thicker continental granite plate

3. MOVE TOWARDS EACH OTHER – Destructive plate margins

- As plates are moving away from each other in some places ...
- ... it follows that they must be MOVING TOWARDS EACH OTHER in other places.
- This results in the THINNER, DENSER, OCEANIC PLATE being FORCED DOWN (SUBDUCTED) beneath ...
- ... the THICKER CONTINENTAL GRANITE PLATE, where it MELTS back into the MAGMA.
- This SUBDUCTION forces continental crust upwards to form MOUNTAINS and even VOLCANOES ...
- ... and EARTHQUAKES are common e.g. West Coast of South America (Andes).
- N.B. Only OCEANIC PLATES are SUBDUCTED(!!!) AND RECYCLED INTO THE MAGMA.

- Tectonic Plates can either slide past each other, move away from each other (constructive plate margins) or move towards each other (destructive plate margins).

1. a) Natural gas is made up mainly of Methane which contains the elements Carbon and Hydrogen only. If Methane is burned.
    a) Which gas from the atmosphere reacts with Methane?
    b) What are the TWO waste products formed during the burning?
    c) Which ONE of the waste products turns limewater milky?

2. a) Name ONE gas which is associated with Global Warming?
    b) Name TWO gases which are associated with Acid Rain?
    c) Name TWO affects of Acid Rain?

3. The pie chart opposite shows the composition of the atmosphere.
    a) Name 'A', 'B', 'C' and 'D'.
    b) What else may also be present in varying small quantities?

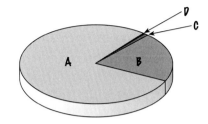

4. The early atmosphere of the Earth was made up mainly of water vapour and three other gases.
    a) Name these gases.
    b) As the first green plants evolved which gas did they take in and which gas did they give out?
    c) Name TWO sources which produced Nitrogen to be released into the atmosphere.
    d) In what way does sea water control the amount of Carbon Dioxide in the atmosphere?

5. Draw and label the diagram opposite using the following words:
    SEDIMENTARY ROCK,
    EXTRUSIVE IGNEOUS ROCK,
    MAGMA,
    INTRUSIVE IGNEOUS ROCK,
    METAMORPHIC ROCK.

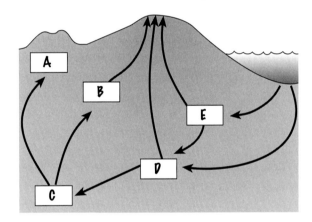

6. a) Explain how (i) sedimentary rocks are formed (ii) igneous rocks are formed.
    b) Which metamorphic rock is made when (i) mudstone experiences extreme temperature and pressure (ii) limestone experiences extreme temperature and pressure.

7. The diagram opposite shows the structure of the Earth.
    a) Name 'A', 'B', 'C' and 'D'.
    b) What evidence is there that 'A' has previously been subjected to very large forces?
    c) What evidence is there that the interior of the Earth is of a different material to 'A'?

8. Fill the spaces below using the following words: HEAT, TECTONIC PLATES, MANTLE, CRUST, RADIOACTIVE DECAY, CONVECTION CURRENTS.
    The Earth's _____ is 'cracked into several large pieces called _____ which move slowly at speeds of a few cm per year driven by _____ in the _____ which are caused by _____ released from _____ .

9. What evidence is there for the 'Tectonic Plates' theory? Explain your answer by comparing the East Coast of South America and the West Coast of Africa.

10. a) What are the consequences of two Tectonic Plates which slide past each other?
    b) Explain how it is possible for two Tectonic Plates to move away from each other.
    c) Explain what happens when two Tectonic Plates move towards each other.

NOTES

NOTES

INDEX

Acid Rain 52
Acids 30, 33, 34
Activation Energy 44, 47
Addition Polymerisation 17
Air 30
Alkali Metals 25, 32
Alkalis 33, 34
Alkanes 16
Alkenes 17
Alloys 29
Aluminium 18, 19
Aluminium, Uses of 29
Aluminium Oxide 19
Ammonia 11, 20, 21, 53
Ammonium Nitrate 20
Aqueous 37
Argon 52
Atmosphere 51, 52, 53
Atoms 8, 10, 26, 27, 37, 38, 39, 42, 43

Basalt 54, 55
Bitumen 16
Blast Furnace 18
Boiling 6
Boiling Point 6, 10, 11, 12, 15, 25, 26
Bond Energies 47
Brine 32
Bromine 7
Burial 55
Burning 46, 52, 53

Calcium 12, 26
Calcium Carbonate 22
Calcium Hydroxide 34
Carbon 13, 15, 16, 17, 18, 19, 39, 53
Carbon Dioxide 18, 45, 46, 51, 52, 53
Carbon Dioxide, Test for 45
Carbon Monoxide 18
Carbonate Rocks 53
Catalyst 20, 21, 28, 44, 45
Change of State 6
Chemical Bonds 47
Chemical Equations 37, 38
Chemical Reactions 37, 38, 44
Chemical Symbols 37
Chlorine 10, 12, 25, 26, 32
Chlorine, Uses of 32
Coal 15
Coke 18
Combustion 46
Compounds 10, 18, 27, 39, 40, 42
Concentration 7, 44, 45
Condensing 6, 16
Conductors 11, 12, 13, 29
Continents 57
Convection Currents 57, 58
Copper 19
Copper, Uses of 29
Core 56

Covalent Bond 10, 11, 13, 16, 17
Covalent Compounds 11, 47
Cracking 16
Crude Oil 15
Crust 56, 57
Cryolite 19
Crystals 54

Denitrifying Bacteria 53
Deposition 55
Diamond 10, 13
Diesel Oil 16
Diffusion 7
Displacement Reactions 31
Dissolving 7
Double Bond 17

Earth 53, 56
Earthquakes 58
Electric Charge 11
Electric Current 19, 43
Electricity 11, 12, 13
Electrodes 19, 32, 43
Electron Configurations 24
Electrons 8, 9, 10, 12, 25, 28
Elements 8, 9, 10, 19, 24, 29, 37, 40, 43
Empirical Formula 42
Endothermic Reactions 46, 47
Energy 6, 47
Energy Level Diagrams 47
Energy Levels 8, 9
Enzymes 45
Erosion 55
Ethane 16
Ethanol 45
Ethene 17
Evaporation 6, 16
Exothermic Reactions 46, 47

Fermentation 45
Fertiliser 20
Forces of Attraction 5, 6, 11, 12
Fossil Fuels 15, 51, 53
Fossils 54, 57
Fractional Distillation 16
Fractionating Column 16
Fractions 16
Freezing 6
Fuel Oil 16
Fuels 16, 46, 52

Gases 5, 6, 7, 15, 29, 32, 37, 42
Giant Structures 10, 12, 13
Global Warming 51
Glucose 45
Gold 18
Granite 54, 55
Graphite 13, 19
Group 0 27, 28

Group 1 25, 28
Group 7 26, 28
Groups 24

Haber Process 20, 21
Half Equations 43
Halogens 26, 32
Hazard Symbols 47
Heat 6, 13, 15, 46, 51, 57, 58
Heat of Reaction 47
Hydrocarbons 15, 18
Hydrochloric Acid 30, 34
Hydrogen 11, 15, 20, 25, 30, 32
Hydrogen, Test for 30
Hydrogen, Uses of 32
Hydrogen Chloride 11
Hydrogen Halides 32

Igneous Rocks 54, 55
Indicators 33
Inert Gases 27
Ionic Bond 10, 12
Ionic Compounds 12, 25, 47
Ionic Salts 26
Ions 12, 13, 19, 43, 47
Iron 18, 20, 21
Iron, Uses of 29
Iron Ore 18
Iron Oxide 18
Isotopes 8

Kinetic Theory 5, 6, 7

Lactic Acid 45
Lattice 13
Limestone 18, 22, 54, 55
Limestone, Uses of 22
Liquids 5, 6, 7, 29, 37
Litmus 33

Magma 54, 55, 58
Magnesium 12
Magnesium Chloride 12
Magnetic Field 58
Mantle 54, 55, 56, 57
Marble 54, 55
Mass Number 8
Melting 6
Melting Point 6, 10, 11, 12, 25, 26, 28
Metal Hydroxides 34
Metal Oxides 34
Metals 12, 13, 18, 24, 25, 26, 29, 31
Metamorphic Rocks 54, 55
Methane 11, 16, 51, 53
Mid Oceanic Ridges 58
Milk 45
Molecules 10, 11, 13, 15, 26, 43
Monatomic 27, 28
Monomers 17

INDEX

Mountains 58
Mud Sediments 15

Naptha 16
Nett Energy Transfers 47
Neutral 33
Neutralisation 20, 33
Neutrons 8
Nitram 20
Nitric Acid 20, 30, 34
Nitrogen 20, 52, 53
Nitrogen Monoxide 20
Nitrogen Oxides 52
Noble Gases 27, 52
Non-Metal Oxides 34
Non-Metals 10, 12, 24, 25, 26, 29
Non-Porous Rock 15
Nucleus 8

Oil 15
Ores 18
Organisms 15
Oxidation 19, 20
Oxides 18, 51
Oxygen 7, 11, 12, 15, 18, 19, 30, 46, 51, 52, 53
Ozone 53
Ozone Layer 53

Paraffin 16
Particles 5, 6, 7
Percentage Mass 40
Periodic Table 24, 29, 37
Periodicity 24
Periods 24
Petrol 16
Petroleum Gas 16
pH Scale 33
Plankton 15
Plants 15
Plastics 13
Plate Margins 58
Platinum 20
Poly(ethene) 16, 17
Polymers 17
Porous Rock 15
Potassium Hydroxide 34
Pressure 15, 20, 21, 42
Products 37, 38, 41, 45, 47
Propane 16
Propene 17
Proton Number 8, 9, 24, 29
Protons 8, 9

Radioactive Decay 57
Rate of Reaction 44, 45
Reactants 37, 38, 41, 44, 45, 47
Reactivity Series 18, 19, 30, 31
Redox Reactions 19
Reduction 18, 19

Relative Atomic Mass 24, 39, 40, 41, 42, 43
Relative Formula Mass 39, 40, 41, 42, 43
Rocks 54, 55, 57

Salt 30, 33
Sandstone 54, 56
Sedimentary Rocks 15, 22, 54, 55, 56
Shells 5, 9, 12, 24, 28
Silicon Dioxide 13
Silver 32
Silver Halides 32
Slag 18
Slate 54, 55
Sodium 12, 25
Sodium Chloride 12, 25, 32
Sodium Hydroxide 32, 34
Sodium Hydroxide, Uses of 32
Solids 5, 6, 7, 29, 37
Solute 7
State Symbols 37
States of Matter 5, 6
Subduction 58
Sulphur 51
Sulphur Dioxide 51, 52
Sulphuric Acid 30, 34
Surface Area 44, 45
Symbols 8

Tectonic Plates 57, 58
Temperature 5, 6, 16, 18, 20, 21, 42, 44, 45, 57, 58
Thermosetting Plastics 13
Thermosoftening Plastics 13
Transition Metals 9, 27
Transportation 55

Universal Indicator 33

Vapours 26
Volcanoes 53, 58
Volume 5, 42, 43

Waste Products 51
Water 11, 15, 20, 25, 30, 33, 46
Water Vapour 51. 52, 53
Weathering 55

Yoghurt Production 45

PERIODIC TABLE OF ELEMENTS

Key

Mass number → 1
Proton number (Atomic number) → 1

| 1 | H hydrogen |

| Group | 1 | 2 | | 3 | 4 | 5 | 6 | 7 | 0 |

									4 He helium 2

| 7 Li lithium 3 | 9 Be beryllium 4 | | | 11 B boron 5 | 12 C carbon 6 | 14 N nitrogen 7 | 16 O oxygen 8 | 19 F fluorine 9 | 20 Ne neon 10 |

| 23 Na sodium 11 | 24 Mg magnesium 12 | | | 27 Al aluminium 13 | 28 Si silicon 14 | 31 P phosphorus 15 | 32 S sulphur 16 | 35 Cl chlorine 17 | 40 Ar argon 18 |

| 39 K potassium 19 | 40 Ca calcium 20 | 45 Sc scandium 21 | 48 Ti titanium 22 | 51 V vanadium 23 | 52 Cr chromium 24 | 55 Mn manganese 25 | 56 Fe iron 26 | 59 Co cobalt 27 | 59 Ni nickel 28 | 63 Cu copper 29 | 64 Zn zinc 30 | 70 Ga gallium 31 | 73 Ge germanium 32 | 75 As arsenic 33 | 79 Se selenium 34 | 80 Br bromine 35 | 84 Kr krypton 36 |

| 85 Rb rubidium 37 | 88 Sr strontium 38 | 89 Y yttrium 39 | 91 Zr zirconium 40 | 93 Nb niobium 41 | 96 Mo molybdenum 42 | 101 Tc technetium 43 | 101 Ru ruthenium 44 | 103 Rh rhodium 45 | 106 Pd palladium 46 | 108 Ag silver 47 | 112 Cd cadmium 48 | 115 In indium 49 | 119 Sn tin 50 | 122 Sb antimony 51 | 128 Te tellurium 52 | 127 I iodine 53 | 131 Xe xenon 54 |

| 133 Cs caesium 55 | 137 Ba barium 56 | 139 La lanthanum 57 | 178 Hf hafnium 72 | 181 Ta tantalum 73 | 184 W tungsten 74 | 186 Re rhenium 75 | 190 Os osmium 76 | 192 Ir iridium 77 | 195 Pt platinum 78 | 197 Au gold 79 | 201 Hg mercury 80 | 204 Tl thallium 81 | 207 Pb lead 82 | 209 Bi bismuth 83 | 210 Po polonium 84 | 210 At astatine 85 | 222 Rn radon 86 |

| 223 Fr francium 87 | 226 Ra radium 88 | 227 Ac actinium 89 |

| 140 Ce cerium 58 | 141 Pr praseodymium 59 | 144 Nd neodymium 60 | 147 Pm promethium 61 | 150 Sm samarium 62 | 152 Eu europium 63 | 157 Gd gadolinium 64 | 159 Tb terbium 65 | 162 Dy dysprosium 66 | 165 Ho holmium 67 | 167 Er erbium 68 | 169 Tm thulium 69 | 173 Yb ytterbium 70 | 175 Lu lutetium 71 |

| 232 Th thorium 90 | 231 Pa protactinium 91 | 238 U uranium 92 | 237 Np neptunium 93 | 242 Pu plutonium 94 | 243 Am americium 95 | 247 Cm curium 96 | 247 Bk berkelium 97 | 251 Cf californium 98 | 254 Es einsteinium 99 | 253 Fm fermium 100 | 256 Md mendelevium 101 | 254 No nobelium 102 | 257 Lw lawrencium 103 |

→ The lines of elements going across are called **periods**.

← The columns of elements going down are called **groups**.